# Heart Healthy Cookbook

Your Guide to Easy and Tasty Heart-Happy Recipes.
Start a Journey of Flavor and Nutrition

**Avery Lynn Morgan**

# 3

**EXTRA BONUS**

## INSIDE THE BOOK

### MEAL PLAN

### GROCERY LIST

### INGREDIENT SWAP CHART

**All printable in FULL COLOR**

Scroll to the end and **SCAN** the **QR CODE**

Table of Contents

# Introduction

Dear Reader,

Welcome to the "Heart Healthy Cookbook for Beginners: Your Guide to Easy and Tasty Heart-Happy Recipes. Start a Journey of Flavour and Nutrition." This book is more than just a compilation of heart-healthy recipes—it's a doorway to a new lifestyle, a roadmap to a journey where your heart leads the way to overall well-being.

The motivation behind penning down this cookbook stems from a blend of personal experiences and the universal need to guide individuals towards a healthier lifestyle. The essence of this book is to make heart-healthy cooking an enjoyable and sustainable practice, not a daunting task. It's about discovering that a heart-healthy diet can be as flavorful and diverse as it is beneficial.

The alarming rise in heart-related ailments globally underscores the importance of a heart-healthy diet. However, transitioning to such a diet can often feel overwhelming, especially with the plethora of information available. This cookbook aims to simplify that transition. It's designed to be your companion as you explore the world of heart-healthy ingredients and delightful recipes that cater to a variety of taste buds.

Inside these pages, you'll find easy-to-follow recipes that require no professional culinary skills, alongside essential nutritional information to help you make informed choices. Whether you are a busy parent, a young professional, or someone venturing into the realm of health-conscious eating, this cookbook is tailored to meet you where you are.

As you delve into the chapters, you'll discover a range of breakfast, lunch, dinner, and snack recipes that are not only nourishing but also pleasing to the palate. Each recipe is accompanied by simple instructions, ingredient lists that are easy to source, and tips to make your cooking process enjoyable.

Furthermore, the additional resources like the 28-day meal plan, shopping guide, and the heart-healthy ingredient swap chart are crafted to provide you with a holistic approach towards achieving a heart-happy lifestyle.

This cookbook is not about adhering to stringent dietary restrictions but embracing a balanced and heart-friendly dietary routine. It's about making small, sustainable changes that have a significant positive impact on your heart health.

So, let's embark on this exciting culinary journey together! A journey where every recipe you try brings you one step closer to a heart-healthy lifestyle. Your adventure of taste, nutrition, and heart wellness begins right here, right now.

With warm wishes for a heart-happy and flavorful journey,


Avery Lynn Morgan

# Chapter 1: Understanding Heart Health

The heart, a ceaseless pump nestled within our chest, orchestrates the rhythm of life. Each beat resonates with the myriad functions that sustain us, making heart health an indispensable aspect of our overall well-being. As we navigate through the modern-day dietary maze, laden with a spectrum of choices, understanding the essence of heart health becomes imperative. This chapter seeks to elucidate the core aspects of heart health, offering a foundational knowledge that will guide you through the subsequent culinary journey awaiting in this cookbook.

## Basic information on heart health

The heart, the indefatigable engine of our being, is a marvel of biological engineering. With each beat, it ushers life-sustaining blood, carrying vital nutrients and oxygen to every cell, fueling the machinery of life. The significance of maintaining a hearty heart transcends beyond mere physical wellness; it's about cultivating a quality of life that allows us to revel in each moment with vitality and joy. This section aims to elucidate the fundamental facets of heart health, providing a stepping stone for a heart-healthy lifestyle.

### The Cardiovascular System: A Lifeline

At the heart of our being lies the cardiovascular system, an intricate network of arteries, veins, and capillaries, with the heart as its diligent pump. This system is the conduit for the essential lifeblood that nourishes every cell, every organ, ensuring the seamless function of the body's myriad processes. Understanding the mechanics of this system is the first stride towards appreciating the essence of heart health.

### The Menace of Heart Disease: Risk Factors

The modern epoch, with its myriad lifestyle challenges, has seen a surge in heart-related ailments. Factors such as hypertension, elevated cholesterol levels, obesity, diabetes, smoking, excessive alcohol consumption, and a sedentary lifestyle are the nefarious culprits often undermining heart health. Each of these factors can be mitigated, if not entirely alleviated, through conscientious lifestyle and dietary amendments.

### The Heart-Healthy Diet: A Cornerstone

A heart-healthy diet is not about stringent restrictions; it's about embracing a balanced, varied diet rich in nutrient-dense foods. It champions the consumption of a plethora of fruits, vegetables, whole grains, lean proteins, and healthy fats, while minimizing the intake of saturated and trans fats, cholesterol, sodium, and added sugars. It's a celebration of flavors and nutrients that nourish the heart and satiate the palate.

### The Vitality of Physical Activity

Physical activity is an unswerving ally of heart health. Regular exercise aids in maintaining a healthy weight, reducing the risk of heart disease by keeping blood pressure, cholesterol, and sugar levels in check. It's not about arduous workouts, but consistent, enjoyable physical activity that resonates with your lifestyle.

### The Prudence of Regular Check-ups

Routine medical check-ups are a prudent measure to monitor and maintain heart health. They provide a window for early detection and management of potential risk factors, ensuring that you stay a step ahead in nurturing your heart's wellness.

### Stress Management: A Silent Guardian

The vicissitudes of modern life often ferry along stress, an insidious foe of heart health. Chronic stress, especially when it fosters detrimental habits like unhealthy eating or smoking, can wreak havoc on heart health. Cultivating healthy stress management techniques is a fortification against the potential adverse impacts on the heart.

### Medication Management: A Guided Approach

For those with pre-existing conditions or risk factors, medication management is a crucial aspect of heart health. Adhering to prescribed medications, following the guidance of healthcare professionals, and regular monitoring ensure that these conditions are well-managed, mitigating risks to heart health.

Armed with this foundational understanding of heart health, you are better poised to embrace the heart-healthy recipes and lifestyle tips that ensue in this cookbook. Each step you take on this culinary journey is a step towards fostering a heart-happy life, brimming with vitality and joy. As you delve into the subsequent chapters, let this foundation guide your voyage through a world of heart-healthy culinary delights, nourishing not just your heart, but your soul.

## Common heart ailments and how diet affects heart health

Heart health is a nuanced and multifaceted aspect of our overall well-being, influenced by a myriad of factors ranging from genetics to lifestyle choices. Among these, diet holds a paramount position, playing a pivotal role in either nurturing or undermining the health of our heart. Before delving into the dietary dimensions, it's crucial to understand some common heart ailments that are prevalent in today's society.

### Atherosclerosis

Atherosclerosis is a pervasive condition characterized by the hardening and narrowing of the arteries due to the accumulation of substances like cholesterol, fat, and cellular waste products on the inner walls of arteries. This accumulation forms plaques, which can either partially or completely block blood flow through these crucial vessels. The condition is often stealthy, commencing during adolescence and potentially progressing unnoticed until later in life when it poses serious threats. When the flow of oxygen-rich blood to organs and other parts of the body is reduced, it can lead to a host of severe complications, including coronary artery disease, carotid artery disease, peripheral artery disease, aneurysms, and chronic kidney disease. Lifestyle modifications, including a heart-healthy diet, regular exercise, and avoidance of tobacco, can significantly mitigate the risks associated with atherosclerosis.

### Coronary Artery Disease (CAD)

Coronary artery disease is a sinister manifestation of atherosclerosis specifically affecting the arteries that supply the heart muscle with blood, oxygen, and nutrients. When these arteries are narrowed or blocked due to plaque buildup, the heart muscle's blood supply is compromised. This can lead to angina, a type of chest pain caused by reduced blood flow to the heart, and myocardial infarctions (heart attacks), where part of the heart muscle is damaged or dies due to lack of blood flow. Early detection, lifestyle modifications, medical management, and in severe cases, surgical interventions, can play a pivotal role in managing CAD and preventing fatal outcomes.

### Hypertension (High Blood Pressure)

It is called hypertension, or high blood pressure, when the force of the blood against the artery walls stays high for a long time. Over time, this heightened pressure can damage the arteries, leading to atherosclerosis, and subsequently, other heart-related conditions. Hypertension is often dubbed as a 'silent killer' due to its asymptomatic nature in the initial stages. Regular monitoring of blood pressure, adhering to a heart-healthy diet low in sodium and rich in potassium, regular physical activity, and prescribed medication management can aid in controlling hypertension and preventing its deleterious effects on heart health.

### Heart Failure

Heart failure is a long-term condition that gets worse over time. It happens when the heart muscle can't pump blood well enough to meet the body's needs for oxygen and blood. The heart is still beating, but not as well as it should. Heart failure can result from conditions that overwork or damage the heart, including hypertension, coronary artery disease, and diabetes. Managing heart failure involves a combination of medication management, lifestyle modifications, and in some cases, surgical interventions to improve the heart's function and quality of life for individuals.

### Arrhythmias

Arrhythmias entail a range of conditions characterized by irregular heartbeats, which can result in the heart pumping too much or too little blood. The irregular heartbeat can lead to a myriad of complications, ranging from fatigue and weakness to heart failure and sudden cardiac arrest if not managed appropriately. Managing and treating arrhythmias depends on the type and severity of the arrhythmia. It may include taking medications, making changes to your lifestyle, or having medical procedures.

### Valvular Heart Diseases

Valvular heart diseases encompass conditions affecting the valves of the heart, which play a crucial role in directing blood flow through the heart's chambers. When the valves don't open or close properly, the disruptions in blood flow can strain the heart and impede its ability to pump blood efficiently. Conditions like stenosis, regurgitation, and atresia are various forms of valvular heart diseases. The management of valvular heart diseases ranges from watchful waiting and medication management to valve repair or replacement surgery in severe cases. Adopting a heart-healthy lifestyle can play a supportive role in managing valvular heart diseases and improving the quality of life for affected individuals.

Now, the nexus between diet and heart health is both profound and intricate. Here's how diet casts its impact:

1. **Cholesterol and Fat Intake:** The types and amount of fat we consume have a direct bearing on our blood cholesterol levels, which in turn significantly affect the risk of coronary artery disease. Fats are not created equal; some can be allies while others foes in our quest for heart health. Unsaturated fats, which you can find in nuts, avocados, and olive oil, can help lower bad cholesterol and raise good cholesterol. On the flip side, saturated fats and trans fats, often found in fried foods, cakes, pies, and certain margarines, can elevate harmful cholesterol levels. Making a heart-healthy choice involves opting for unsaturated fats while minimizing the intake of saturated and trans fats. This subtle shift in dietary choice can lead to a profound positive impact on heart health.

2. **Sodium Consumption:** Sodium is a necessary mineral for body function, yet an excess intake is a known protagonist for hypertension or high blood pressure—a condition that strains the heart over time. The modern diet is often laden with hidden sodium, tucked away in processed foods, canned goods, and restaurant fare. A heart-healthy diet emphasizes reducing sodium intake, which can significantly aid in maintaining a healthy blood pressure and in turn, a hearty heart. Opting for fresh, unprocessed foods and being mindful of the sodium content in the foods you consume can pave the way towards better heart health.

3. **Fiber-Rich Diet:** Dietary fiber is a heart's good friend. It has the remarkable ability to lower bad cholesterol levels, thus reducing the risk of heart disease. A diet rich in fiber is often synonymous with a repertoire of whole grains, fruits, vegetables, and legumes—a colorful, varied diet that tantalizes the palate while nurturing the heart. The heart-healthy recipes in this cookbook celebrate the essence of a fiber-rich diet, guiding you towards making choices that satiate not just your hunger, but your heart's health needs.

4. **Antioxidant-Rich Foods:** Antioxidants are the valiant knights that combat oxidative stress, a nefarious process implicated in heart disease and other ailments. An imbalance between free radicals and antioxidants in the body is what oxidative stress is all about. This can damage cells and tissues. Foods rich in antioxidants like berries, nuts, spinach, and artichokes help to combat this imbalance, promoting heart health. Incorporating a variety of antioxidant-rich foods in your diet is akin to arming your body with a protective shield against heart disease.

5. **Lean Proteins:** Proteins are essential building blocks for our body, yet the source of protein can significantly impact heart health. Lean proteins, such as poultry, fish, legumes, and low-fat dairy products, provide the necessary nutrients without excessive saturated and trans fats. Reducing the intake of red or processed meats, which are often high in unhealthy fats, while embracing lean proteins, forms a dietary strategy conducive to heart health.

6. **Omega-3 Fatty Acids:** Omega-3 fatty acids are the virtuous fats known for their heart-healthy benefits. They have been shown to lower the risk of heart disease, reduce inflammation, and lower bad cholesterol levels. Foods rich in omega-3 fatty acids like fish, walnuts, and flaxseeds are beneficial additions to a heart-healthy diet. The recipes in this cookbook introduce a variety of ways to incorporate these beneficial fats into your daily meals.

7. **Alcohol Moderation:** Alcohol, when consumed in moderation, might have certain health benefits. However, excessive alcohol consumption is a known adversary to heart health, leading to high blood pressure, heart failure, and even stroke. Moderation in alcohol intake is not just a prudent choice; it's a heart-healthy choice. Being mindful of alcohol consumption is an essential aspect of fostering a heart-healthy lifestyle.

8. **Maintaining a Healthy Weight:** A balanced diet and regular physical activity are the stalwarts of achieving and maintaining a healthy weight—a critical aspect of heart health. Excess weight often heralds a host of other conditions like high blood pressure, high cholesterol levels, and diabetes, which are detrimental to heart health.

Understanding the common heart ailments and the dietary factors that affect heart health provides a lens through which one can appreciate the heart-healthy recipes presented in this cookbook. As you peruse through the delectable recipes, each ingredient chosen and every meal prepared is a step towards fostering a heart-healthy lifestyle, mitigating the risks of heart ailments, and paving the way towards a vibrant, hearty life.

# Chapter 2:    Nutritional Foundations

## Basic nutritional information

Embarking on a heart-healthy culinary journey entails a fundamental understanding of nutritional concepts that underline the essence of a balanced diet. Nutrition is a vast field, but at its core, it revolves around the macronutrients and micronutrients that are vital for our bodies to function optimally. This section aims to provide a succinct overview of basic nutritional information, forming a springboard for making informed dietary choices conducive to heart health.

## Macronutrients

### Carbohydrates:

- For the body, carbohydrates are the main source of energy.
- They are categorized into simple (sugars) and complex (starches and fibers) carbohydrates.
- It is better for your heart to eat complex carbs like whole grains, legumes, and vegetables instead of refined grains and sugars.

### Proteins:

- Proteins are essential for tissue repair, immune function, and muscle building.
- Sources include animal products like meat and dairy, and plant-based sources like legumes and nuts.
- Opting for lean proteins and plant-based proteins can contribute to a heart-healthy diet.

### Fats:

- Fats are crucial for cell structure, hormone production, and nutrient absorption.
- They are categorized into saturated, unsaturated, and trans fats.
- Unsaturated fats (monounsaturated and polyunsaturated fats) found in olive oil, avocados, and nuts are heart-healthy choices, while trans fats and saturated fats should be minimized.

## Micronutrients

### Vitamins and Minerals:

- These are vital for a plethora of bodily functions including energy production, immune function, and bone health.
- A balanced diet rich in a variety of fruits, vegetables, whole grains, lean proteins, and healthy fats generally provides an adequate amount of vitamins and minerals.

### Antioxidants:

- Antioxidants like vitamin C, vitamin E, and selenium combat oxidative stress, which can contribute to heart disease.
- They are abundantly found in fruits, vegetables, nuts, and seeds.

## Fiber

- Dietary fiber, though not digestible, plays a significant role in heart health by helping to lower cholesterol levels and promoting a healthy gut.

## Water

- Water is the cornerstone of life, crucial for every cellular function, including those of the heart and brain. Adequate hydration is essential for overall health.

## Understanding Nutrient Labels

- Being able to decipher nutrient labels on food packaging can empower you to make heart-healthy dietary choices. Look for lower levels of saturated fats, trans fats, cholesterol, and sodium, and higher levels of dietary fiber.

As you delve into the heart-healthy recipes in the subsequent chapters, this foundational understanding of nutrition will guide your choices, enabling you to select ingredients that not only tantalize your taste buds but also nurture your heart. Each recipe is a step towards a harmonious balance of flavors and nutrients, paving the path towards a hearty, nourishing culinary adventure.

## Foods that are heart-healthy

Embarking on a heart-healthy dietary journey is akin to forging a nurturing relationship with the myriad foods that not only satiate our taste buds but also cater to our heart's wellbeing. This section unveils a palette of foods celebrated for their heart-healthy attributes, each bringing a unique blend of nutrients and flavors to your table. These foods, when integrated into a balanced diet, contribute to a heart-friendly lifestyle that resonates with vitality and wholesomeness.

### Fruits and Vegetables

**Berries:** Berries are rich in antioxidants, vitamins, and minerals that help combat oxidative stress and inflammation, both of which are linked to heart disease.

**Leafy Greens:** Spinach, kale, and other leafy greens are high in vitamins, minerals, and antioxidants, particularly vitamin K, which is essential for maintaining healthy arteries and blood clotting.

### Whole Grains

**Oats, Quinoa, and Barley:** These grains are rich in fiber, which can help lower cholesterol levels and support heart health.

### Lean Proteins

**Fish:** Omega-3 fatty acids are found in large amounts in fatty fish like salmon and mackerel. These acids are known to lower blood pressure and lower the risk of heart disease.

**Poultry:** Chicken and turkey are lean proteins that, when consumed in moderation and cooked in a healthy manner, can be part of a heart-healthy diet.

### Healthy Fats

**Avocados:** These are loaded with monounsaturated fats and potassium, known for lowering bad cholesterol levels and promoting heart health.

**Olive Oil:** A staple in the Mediterranean diet, olive oil is rich in antioxidants and monounsaturated fats that promote heart health.

### Nuts and Seeds

**Almonds, Walnuts, and Chia Seeds:** These are rich in fiber, vitamins, and omega-3 fatty acids, which are beneficial for heart health.

### Legumes

**Beans, Lentils, and Peas:** They are excellent sources of protein, fiber, and numerous vitamins and minerals, promoting a healthy heart.

### Dairy Alternatives

**Almond Milk, Soy Milk:** These plant-based milk alternatives are often lower in saturated fats compared to traditional dairy, making them heart-healthy choices.

### Herbs and Spices

**Garlic, Turmeric:** These spices have been linked to lower cholesterol levels and reduced risk of heart disease.

Embracing a diverse range of heart-healthy foods is not only a culinary exploration but a venture into a lifestyle that cherishes heart health. The ensuing chapters will introduce you to a plethora of recipes that celebrate these heart-healthy foods in a medley of flavors, textures, and aromas. As you traverse through these recipes, each meal you prepare is a tribute to your heart, a step towards a life brimming with health, energy, and joy.

# Portion control and balanced meals

Navigating the realm of heart-healthy eating also necessitates a keen understanding of portion control and the essence of balanced meals. It's not just about what you eat, but how much you eat and how well-rounded your meals are. This section endeavors to provide insights into cultivating a mindful approach towards portion control and embracing the harmony of balanced meals, both of which are instrumental in fostering heart health.

## Portion Control
### Understanding Serving Sizes:

- Grasping the concept of serving sizes helps in moderating the quantity of food consumed. Utilizing measuring cups and food scales can be useful tools in this regard.

### Mindful Eating:

- Be more mindful by eating slowly, enjoying every bite, and paying attention to your body's signals for when it's hungry and when it's full. This promotes better portion control and a more enjoyable eating experience.

## Balanced Meals
### Incorporating a Variety of Nutrients:

- A balanced meal is a colorful palette of various nutrients—carbohydrates, proteins, fats, vitamins, and minerals. This diversity not only nurtures your heart but also your overall well-being.

### Harmonizing Macronutrients:

- Aim for a harmony of macronutrients—carbohydrates for energy, proteins for muscle repair and growth, and healthy fats for cell function and satiety.

### Including a Rainbow of Fruits and Vegetables:

- The different colors in fruits and vegetables represent different nutrients; incorporating a variety ensures you're receiving a broad spectrum of nutrients beneficial for heart health.

## Practical Tips
### Utilizing Smaller Plates and Bowls:

- Smaller dishware can help in serving and consuming smaller portions, aiding in portion control without feeling deprived.

### Dividing Your Plate:

- A helpful strategy is to divide your plate into sections—half for vegetables, a quarter for protein, and a quarter for whole grains or complex carbohydrates.

## Monitoring and Adjusting
### Regular Monitoring:

- Keeping a food diary or using food tracking apps can provide insights into your portion sizes and meal balance, helping you make necessary adjustments.

### Seeking Professional Guidance:

- If needed, consulting with a registered dietitian can provide personalized guidance on portion control and balanced meals aligned with your heart-healthy goals.

Embracing portion control and the art of balanced meals is a nurturing pathway towards heart health. It cultivates a mindful, informed approach towards eating, where each meal becomes an opportunity to nourish your heart and soul. The subsequent recipes and meal plans in this cookbook are designed with this ethos in mind, guiding you through a culinary journey that is as heart-healthy as it is delightful and satisfying. Through this heart-healthy lens, the act of eating transforms into a joyful celebration of life, love, and good health.

# Chapter 3:   Getting Started

## Kitchen essentials for heart-healthy cooking

Stepping into a heart-friendly culinary journey calls for having the right tools and essentials at your disposal. A well-equipped kitchen is like a canvas ready for a painter, allowing you to explore, experiment, and create meals that not only satiate your taste buds but also nurture your heart. From quality cookware that ensures even cooking and retains the nutritional value of your ingredients, to handy gadgets that make the preparation of heart-friendly meals more efficient and enjoyable, having the right kitchen essentials is pivotal. This section endeavors to provide a curated list of kitchen tools, gadgets, and essentials that will be your allies in crafting heart-friendly meals. Whether you're a seasoned chef or a beginner in the kitchen, having the right tools can significantly enhance your cooking experience, making the path to heart-friendly eating an enjoyable and rewarding venture.

### Quality Cookware
#### Material Matters:

- Opt for materials like stainless steel, cast iron, or ceramic that not only ensure even cooking but are also durable and free from harmful chemicals.

- Non-stick pans with a ceramic coating can be a healthier choice, allowing for less oil usage while cooking.

#### Versatile Pieces:

- Investing in versatile cookware like a good quality dutch oven or a multi-functional pressure cooker can be beneficial. They provide the flexibility to cook a variety of heart-healthy meals, from soups to stews and braised dishes.

### Handy Gadgets
#### Efficiency Enhancers:

- Gadgets like food processors, blenders, and hand-held immersion blenders can significantly cut down preparation time, making it easier to whip up heart-healthy meals even on busy days.

#### Precision Tools:

- Tools like digital scales and measuring cups aid in ensuring precise ingredient quantities, which is crucial for adhering to heart-healthy recipes and portion control.

### Essential Utensils
#### Mindful Selection:

- Opt for utensils that promote healthy cooking, like steaming baskets for preserving nutrients, and silicone spatulas that are gentle on your cookware and free from harmful chemicals.

#### Organization is Key:

- Having a well-organized utensil drawer or holder makes the cooking process smoother, ensuring you have the right tools readily accessible.

### Pantry Essentials
#### Heart-Healthy Staples:

- Stock your pantry with heart-healthy staples like whole grains, legumes, nuts, seeds, and a variety of herbs and spices. Having these essentials on hand encourages the preparation of nutritious meals.

#### Ingredient Swaps:

- Keep a list of heart-healthy ingredient swaps handy. For instance, swapping out saturated fats with unsaturated fats like olive oil can make a significant difference in your heart health.

Creating a kitchen environment that is primed for heart-healthy cooking is a step towards making heart health a tangible, enjoyable, and sustainable aspect of your daily life. Each tool, gadget, and essential item in your kitchen is a companion on this heart-healthy culinary journey, making the process of cooking not just a routine, but a delightful venture into the world of nutritious and wholesome eating.

## Tips for grocery shopping for heart-healthy ingredients

Venturing into the aisles of a grocery store can initially feel like navigating a labyrinth, especially when you're dedicated to embarking on a heart-healthy culinary journey. The plethora of choices can be overwhelming, yet with a dash of preparation and a sprinkle of knowledge, you can make choices that are kind to your heart and tantalizing to your taste buds. Here are some enriched tips to guide you through a heart-healthy grocery shopping experience:

1. **Prepare a List:**

   - A well-thought-out list is your best companion. Before you set foot in the store, draft a list of heart-healthy ingredients you'll need. This not only streamlines your shopping experience, saving time, but also acts as a compass, keeping you aligned with your heart-healthy goals.

2. **Shop the Perimeter:**

   - Fresh fruits and vegetables, lean meats, and dairy products are usually kept around the outside of the store. Begin your shopping expedition here to load your cart with heart-healthy staples that form the base of a nutritious diet.

3. **Read Labels:**

   - The labels on products are tales of what's inside. Take a moment to read nutrition labels, hunting for low sodium, low saturated fat, and zero trans fat products. Keep an eye out for added sugars and aim for products with simple, recognizable ingredients.

4. **Opt for Whole Grains:**

   - Whole grains are a treasure trove of nutrients. Choose whole grains over refined ones. Look for whole wheat, brown rice, quinoa, and other whole-grain warriors.

5. **Select Lean Proteins:**

   - Lean proteins are your allies in building a heart-healthy meal plan. Opt for poultry, fish, legumes, and nuts. When possible, choose grass-fed or organic meats to dodge unwanted additives.

6. **Go for Healthy Fats:**

   - Healthy fats are crucial for a balanced diet. Include avocados, nuts, seeds, and olive oil in your shopping arsenal.

7. **Choose Fresh or Frozen Produce:**

   - Fresh or frozen fruits and vegetables are usually devoid of added sugars or sodium, making them a healthier choice. They are the knights in shining armor in your heart-healthy culinary quest.

8. **Avoid Processed Foods:**

   - The aisles laden with heavily processed foods are where you need to steer clear. These often house unhealthy fats, added sugars, and high levels of sodium.

9. **Consider Online Shopping:**

   - In the digital age, online grocery shopping is a boon. If physical stores are overwhelming or time is of the essence, online shopping can be a heart-healthy haven. Many online platforms now parade a wide range of healthy food options delivered right to your doorstep.

10. **Utilize Health-Focused Apps:**

    - Embrace the aid of technology with health-focused apps. They can assist in identifying heart-healthy products, comparing nutrition labels, and even offering healthy recipe suggestions tailored to the items you've bagged.

11. **Seek Seasonal and Local:**

    - Local and seasonal food not only helps local farmers, but it's also fresher and full of the best nutrients.

12. **Practice Mindful Shopping:**

    - Lastly, practice mindfulness as you shop. Take it as an opportunity to make conscious choices that favor your heart's wellbeing and echo your commitment to a healthier lifestyle.

Equipped with these enriched tips and a well-prepared shopping list, your ventures to the grocery store can morph from being a chore to a more purposeful and enjoyable expedition, propelling you further along on your heart-healthy culinary voyage.

# Chapter 4:    Breakfast Recipes

## 1.  Oat Pancakes

**Prep Time:** 10 minutes | **Cooking Time:** 15 minutes | **Serving Size:** 4

**Ingredients**

- 1 cup rolled oats
- 1/2 cup whole wheat flour
- 2 teaspoons baking powder
- 1/2 teaspoon salt
- 1 tablespoon honey or maple syrup
- 1 cup unsweetened almond milk
- 2 large eggs
- 1 teaspoon vanilla extract
- Cooking spray or olive oil, for cooking

**Instructions**

1. Place the rolled oats in a blender or food processor and blend until they reach a fine, flour-like consistency.
2. In a large mixing bowl, combine the oat flour, whole wheat flour, baking powder, and salt.
3. In a separate bowl, whisk together the honey or maple syrup, almond milk, eggs, and vanilla extract until well combined.
4. Pour the wet ingredients into the dry ingredients and stir gently until just combined. Be careful not to over-mix, as this can make the pancakes tough.
5. Heat a non-stick skillet or griddle over medium heat and lightly coat with cooking spray or a small amount of olive oil.
6. Pour 1/4 cup of the batter onto the skillet for each pancake and cook for 2-3 minutes on each side or until the pancakes are golden brown and cooked through.
7. Serve warm with your choice of heart-healthy toppings such as fresh berries, a dollop of Greek yogurt, or a drizzle of maple syrup.

**Nutritional Information:**

160 Calories - 25g Carbs - 3g Fat - 1g Saturated Fats - 6g Protein - 3g Fibers - 220mg Sodium - 5g Sugar

**Tip:**

- Adding a handful of fresh blueberries or banana slices to the batter can provide an extra burst of flavor and nutrients.

**Nutritional Benefits:**

- Protein-Packed: Eggs provide a good amount of protein which is essential for muscle repair and growth.

## 2. Sunrise Berry Quinoa Bowl

**Prep Time:** 10 minutes | **Cooking Time:** 20 minutes | **Serving Size:** 2

**Ingredients**

- 1/2 cup quinoa, rinsed and drained
- 1 cup water
- 1/2 cup fresh blueberries
- 1/2 cup fresh strawberries, hulled and halved
- 1/4 cup almonds, sliced
- 1 tablespoon chia seeds
- 1 tablespoon honey or maple syrup
- 1/2 teaspoon cinnamon (optional)
- 1/4 cup unsweetened almond milk

**Instructions**

1. In a medium saucepan, bring the quinoa and water to a boil over high heat. Once boiling, reduce heat to low, cover, and simmer for 15-20 minutes, or until quinoa is cooked and water is absorbed.
2. While the quinoa is cooking, prepare the berries and almonds.
3. Once the quinoa is cooked, fluff it with a fork and divide it between two bowls.
4. Top each bowl with equal amounts of blueberries, strawberries, almonds, and chia seeds.
5. Drizzle with honey or maple syrup, sprinkle with cinnamon if using, and pour almond milk over the top.
6. Serve immediately, or cover and refrigerate to enjoy cold later.

**Nutritional Information:**

230 Calories - 35g Carbs - 7g Fat - 0.5g Saturated Fats - 8g Protein - 6g Fibers - 60mg Sodium - 10g Sugar

**Tip:**

- You can cook the quinoa in advance to save time in the morning.

**Nutritional Benefits:**

- Protein and Fiber Rich: Quinoa is a complete protein providing all nine essential amino acids, and is also high in fiber which promotes good digestion.

# 3. Nutty Banana Muffins

**Prep Time:** 15 minutes | **Cooking Time:** 20 minutes | **Serving Size:** 12 muffins

## Ingredients

- 1 1/2 cups whole wheat flour
- 1/2 cup rolled oats
- 2 teaspoons baking powder
- 1/2 teaspoon baking soda
- 1/4 teaspoon salt
- 1/2 cup unsweetened applesauce
- 1/4 cup honey or maple syrup
- 2 ripe bananas, mashed
- 1/4 cup unsweetened almond milk
- 2 large eggs
- 1 teaspoon vanilla extract
- 1/2 cup walnuts, chopped

## Instructions

1. Preheat the oven to 350°F (175°C) and line a muffin tin with paper liners or lightly grease with cooking spray.
2. In a large bowl, combine the whole wheat flour, rolled oats, baking powder, baking soda, and salt.
3. In a separate bowl, mix together the applesauce, honey or maple syrup, mashed bananas, almond milk, eggs, and vanilla extract until well combined.
4. Gradually add the wet ingredients to the dry ingredients, stirring gently until just combined. Fold in the walnuts.
5. Divide the batter evenly among the muffin cups, filling each about 2/3 full.
6. Bake for 18-20 minutes, or until a toothpick inserted into the center of a muffin comes out clean.
7. Allow muffins to cool in the tin for 5 minutes, then transfer to a wire rack to cool completely.

## Nutritional Information:

150 Calories - 25g Carbs - 4g Fat - 0.5g Saturated Fats - 5g Protein - 3g Fibers - 150mg Sodium - 9g Sugar

**Tip:**

- Store leftover muffins in an airtight container at room temperature for up to 2 days, or freeze for up to 3 months.

**Nutritional Benefits:**

- Heart-Healthy Fats: Walnuts are rich in omega-3 fatty acids which are known for their heart-healthy benefits.

# 4. Avocado Toast with Sunflower Seeds

**Prep Time:** 10 minutes | **Cooking Time:** 5 minutes | **Serving Size:** 2

**Ingredients**

- 1 ripe avocado
- 2 slices of whole-grain bread
- 1 tablespoon sunflower seeds
- 1 teaspoon lemon juice
- Salt and black pepper to taste
- Optional toppings: radish slices, cherry tomatoes, fresh herbs (like cilantro or parsley)

**Instructions**

1. Toast the slices of whole-grain bread to your liking.
2. While the bread is toasting, pit and peel the avocado, then mash it in a bowl. Stir in the lemon juice, salt, and black pepper.
3. Spread the mashed avocado evenly over each slice of toasted bread.
4. Sprinkle sunflower seeds on top of the avocado spread.
5. If desired, top with radish slices, cherry tomatoes, and/or fresh herbs.
6. Serve immediately and enjoy.

**Nutritional Information:**

250 Calories - 18g Carbs - 20g Fat - 3g Saturated Fats - 6g Protein - 9g Fibers - 150mg Sodium - 3g Sugar

**Tip:**

- Feel free to customize with other toppings like a poached egg, or a sprinkle of nutritional yeast for a cheesy flavor.

**Nutritional Benefits:**

- Nutrient Dense: Sunflower seeds are a great source of vitamins and minerals including Vitamin E, an antioxidant beneficial for heart health.

# 5. Cardio Kickstart Smoothie Bowl

**Prep Time:** 10 minutes | **Cooking Time:** 0 minutes | **Serving Size:** 1

**Ingredients**

- 1/2 cup unsweetened almond milk
- 1/2 banana, frozen
- 1/2 cup mixed berries, frozen
- 1 tablespoon chia seeds
- 1 tablespoon almond butter
- 1/4 cup granola
- 1 tablespoon shredded coconut
- Additional toppings: fresh berries, nuts, seeds

**Instructions**

1. In a blender, combine the almond milk, frozen banana, mixed berries, chia seeds, and almond butter. Blend until smooth and creamy.
2. Pour the smoothie mixture into a bowl.
3. Top with granola, shredded coconut, and any additional toppings you desire.
4. Serve immediately and enjoy.

**Nutritional Information:**

350 Calories - 45g Carbs - 17g Fat - 2g Saturated Fats - 10g Protein - 13g Fibers - 150mg Sodium - 18g Sugar

**Tip:**

- For a thicker smoothie bowl, add more frozen fruit or less almond milk.

**Nutritional Benefits:**

- Antioxidant Rich: Berries are loaded with antioxidants, which help your body fight oxidative stress caused by free radical.

# 6. Morning Glory Granola

**Prep Time:** 10 minutes | **Cooking Time:** 25 minutes | **Serving Size:** 10 servings

**Ingredients**

- 2 cups old-fashioned rolled oats
- 1/2 cup unsweetened shredded coconut
- 1/2 cup almonds, chopped
- 1/4 cup sunflower seeds
- 1/4 cup pumpkin seeds
- 1/4 cup dried cranberries or raisins
- 1/4 cup maple syrup or honey
- 2 tablespoons coconut oil, melted
- 1 teaspoon vanilla extract

- 1/2 teaspoon cinnamon
- 1/4 teaspoon salt

**Instructions**

1. Preheat your oven to 325°F (160°C). Line a baking sheet with parchment paper.

2. In a large mixing bowl, combine the oats, shredded coconut, almonds, sunflower seeds, pumpkin seeds, and dried cranberries or raisins.

3. In a separate small bowl, whisk together the maple syrup or honey, melted coconut oil, vanilla extract, cinnamon, and salt until well combined.

4. Pour the liquid mixture over the dry ingredients and stir well to coat evenly.

5. Spread the granola mixture onto the prepared baking sheet in an even layer.

6. Bake for 20-25 minutes, stirring halfway through, until the granola is golden brown and crispy.

7. Allow the granola to cool completely on the baking sheet before storing in an airtight container for up to 2 weeks.

**Nutritional Information:**

200 Calories - 20g Carbs - 12g Fat - 4g Saturated Fats - 5g Protein - 4g Fibers - 60mg Sodium - 9g Sugar

**Tip:**

- Serve this granola with a splash of milk or a dollop of yogurt for a heart-healthy breakfast.

**Nutritional Benefits:**

- Low in Saturated Fat: This granola is low in saturated fats which is beneficial for maintaining healthy cholesterol levels.

## 7. Omega-Boosting Chia Pudding

**Prep Time:** 5 minutes | **Cooking Time:** 0 minutes (plus 2 hours refrigeration) | **Serving Size:** 2

**Ingredients**

- 1/4 cup chia seeds
- 1 cup unsweetened almond milk
- 1 tablespoon maple syrup or honey
- 1/2 teaspoon vanilla extract
- Toppings: Fresh berries, nuts, and a drizzle of honey

**Instructions**

1. In a medium-sized mixing bowl, combine the chia seeds, almond milk, maple syrup or honey, and vanilla extract. Stir well to combine.

2. Cover the bowl and refrigerate for at least 2 hours, or overnight, until the mixture thickens to a pudding-like consistency.

3. Give the pudding a good stir before dividing between two bowls.

4. Top with fresh berries, nuts, and a drizzle of honey, if desired.

5. Serve immediately and enjoy.

**Nutritional Information:**

180 Calories - 19g Carbs - 10g Fat - 1g Saturated Fats - 6g Protein - 11g Fibers - 90mg Sodium - 8g Sugar

**Tip:**

- For a creamier texture, blend the chia pudding in a blender until smooth before serving.

**Nutritional Benefits:**

- Omega-3 Fatty Acids: Chia seeds are an excellent source of omega-3 fatty acids, which are essential for heart health.

# 8. Oatmeal with Berries

**Prep Time:** 5 minutes | **Cooking Time:** 10 minutes | **Serving Size:** 2

**Ingredients**

- 1 cup old-fashioned rolled oats
- 2 cups water or milk of choice
- 1/2 cup fresh or frozen berries (strawberries, blueberries, raspberries)
- 1 tablespoon chia seeds
- 1-2 tablespoons maple syrup or honey, to taste
- 1/4 teaspoon cinnamon
- Toppings: Additional berries, nuts, seeds

**Instructions**

1. In a medium saucepan, bring the water or milk to a boil.
2. Stir in the rolled oats, reduce heat to low, and simmer for about 10 minutes, or until the oats are tender and have absorbed the liquid.
3. Stir in the berries, chia seeds, maple syrup or honey, and cinnamon.
4. Cook for an additional 2-3 minutes, or until the berries are warmed through.
5. Divide the oatmeal between two bowls and top with additional berries, nuts, and seeds if desired.
6. Serve warm and enjoy.

**Nutritional Information:**

220 Calories - 40g Carbs - 4g Fat - 1g Saturated Fats - 6g Protein - 7g Fibers - 10mg Sodium - 12g Sugar

**Tip:**

- Customize your oatmeal with different toppings like sliced banana, a dollop of yogurt, or a sprinkle of granola.

**Nutritional Benefits:**

- Whole Grain Goodness: Rolled oats are a wholesome grain that can help reduce cholesterol and promote heart health.

# 9. Veggie-Packed Breakfast Burritos

**Prep Time:** 15 minutes | **Cooking Time:** 10 minutes | **Serving Size:** 4

## Ingredients

- 4 whole-grain tortillas
- 4 large eggs, beaten
- 1/4 cup skim milk
- Salt and black pepper, to taste
- 1 tablespoon olive oil
- 1/2 cup diced bell peppers
- 1/4 cup diced onions
- 1/4 cup diced tomatoes
- 1/4 cup shredded low-fat cheddar cheese
- Optional: Salsa, avocado slices, and fresh cilantro for serving

## Instructions

1. In a medium bowl, whisk together the eggs, skim milk, salt, and black pepper. Set aside.
2. Heat olive oil in a non-stick skillet over medium heat.
3. Add the bell peppers and onions to the skillet and sauté for about 3-4 minutes, or until they are soft.
4. Pour the egg mixture over the veggies and let cook for about 1-2 minutes, then gently stir to create soft curds. Continue cooking until the eggs are set but still moist.
5. Warm the tortillas in the oven or on the stovetop.
6. Divide the egg and veggie mixture among the tortillas, then sprinkle with diced tomatoes and shredded cheese.
7. Roll up each tortilla to form a burrito. Serve immediately with optional toppings like salsa, avocado slices, and fresh cilantro.

## Nutritional Information:

280 Calories - 28g Carbs - 12g Fat - 3g Saturated Fats - 14g Protein - 4g Fibers - 540mg Sodium - 4g Sugar

## Tip:

- Prep the veggies the night before to make your morning routine faster.

## Nutritional Benefits:

- Veggie Boost: This burrito is a tasty way to get more veggies into your morning meal.

# 10. Almond Joy Smoothie

**Prep Time:** 5 minutes | **Cooking Time:** 0 minutes | **Serving Size:** 2

## Ingredients

- 1 banana, frozen
- 1/2 cup unsweetened almond milk
- 1/4 cup unsweetened shredded coconut
- 2 tablespoons almond butter
- 1 tablespoon unsweetened cocoa powder
- 1/2 teaspoon vanilla extract
- Ice cubes, as needed
- Optional: 1-2 teaspoons honey or maple syrup for sweetness

## Instructions

1. In a blender, combine the banana, almond milk, shredded coconut, almond butter, cocoa powder, and vanilla extract.
2. Blend on high until smooth and creamy, adding ice cubes as needed to reach your desired consistency.
3. Taste and add honey or maple syrup if desired for additional sweetness.
4. Divide the smoothie between two glasses and serve immediately.

## Nutritional Information:

250 Calories - 18g Carbs - 18g Fat - 3g Saturated Fats - 6g Protein - 6g Fibers - 90mg Sodium - 8g Sugar

## Tip:

- For a thicker smoothie, add more ice cubes or use a frozen banana.

## Nutritional Benefits:

- Natural Sweetness: This smoothie is naturally sweetened with banana, but you can add a little honey or maple syrup if you prefer it sweeter.

# 11. Wholesome Heart Egg White Omelette

**Prep Time:** 10 minutes | **Cooking Time:** 10 minutes | **Serving Size:** 2

## Ingredients

- 1 cup egg whites
- Salt and black pepper, to taste
- 1/2 cup diced tomatoes
- 1/4 cup diced bell peppers
- 1/4 cup diced mushrooms
- 1/4 cup shredded low-fat mozzarella cheese
- 1 tablespoon olive oil
- Fresh herbs such as parsley or chives for garnish

## Instructions

1. In a medium mixing bowl, whisk the egg whites with a pinch of salt and black pepper until slightly frothy.
2. Heat olive oil in a non-stick skillet over medium heat.
3. Add the diced tomatoes, bell peppers, and mushrooms to the skillet, sautéing for 3-4 minutes or until the vegetables are tender.
4. Pour the egg whites over the vegetables and cook without stirring for about 2-3 minutes, or until the edges start to set.
5. Sprinkle the shredded mozzarella cheese on top of the egg whites.
6. Gently fold the omelette in half using a spatula, and let it cook for an additional 2-3 minutes, or until the cheese is melted and the egg whites are fully cooked.
7. Slide the omelette onto a plate, garnish with fresh herbs, slice in half, and serve immediately.

## Nutritional Information:

150 Calories - 5g Carbs - 8g Fat - 2g Saturated Fats - 18g Protein - 1g Fibers - 370mg Sodium - 3g Sugar

## Tip:

- Use fresh herbs to enhance the flavor without adding extra calories or sodium.

## Nutritional Benefits:

- Low Calorie: This omelette is a low-calorie option packed with protein and veggies to start your day on a healthy note.

# 12. Berry-Nut Yogurt Parfait

**Prep Time:** 10 minutes | **Cooking Time:** 0 minutes | **Serving Size:** 2

**Ingredients**

- 1 cup low-fat Greek yogurt
- 1/2 cup fresh mixed berries (strawberries, blueberries, raspberries)
- 2 tablespoons honey or maple syrup
- 1/4 cup granola
- 2 tablespoons chopped nuts (almonds, walnuts, or pecans)

**Instructions**

1. In a medium bowl, gently mix the Greek yogurt with honey or maple syrup until well combined.
2. In serving glasses or bowls, layer half of the yogurt mixture, followed by a layer of granola, and then a layer of mixed berries.
3. Repeat the layers using the remaining yogurt, granola, and berries.
4. Top each parfait with chopped nuts.
5. Serve immediately or refrigerate for up to 2 hours before serving.

**Nutritional Information:**

250 Calories - 35g Carbs - 7g Fat - 1g Saturated Fats - 15g Protein - 3g Fibers - 45mg Sodium - 25g Sugar

**Tip:**

- Choose a low-sugar granola to keep the sugar content in check.

**Nutritional Benefits:**

- Protein Power: Greek yogurt provides a good amount of protein that helps in muscle building and keeping you satiated.

# 13. Tender Loving Care Bran Muffins

**Prep Time:** 15 minutes | **Cooking Time:** 20 minutes | **Serving Size:** 12 muffins

**Ingredients**

- 1 1/2 cups wheat bran
- 1 cup buttermilk
- 1/3 cup vegetable oil
- 1 large egg
- 2/3 cup brown sugar
- 1/2 teaspoon vanilla extract
- 1 cup all-purpose flour
- 1 teaspoon baking soda
- 1 teaspoon baking powder
- 1/2 teaspoon salt

- 1/2 cup raisins

**Instructions**

1. Preheat your oven to 375°F (190°C). Grease muffin cups or line with paper muffin liners.
2. Mix together wheat bran and buttermilk; let stand for 10 minutes.
3. Beat together oil, egg, sugar, and vanilla and add to the bran/buttermilk mixture.
4. Sift together flour, baking soda, baking powder, and salt. Stir flour mixture into bran mixture, until just blended.
5. Fold in raisins and spoon batter into prepared muffin tins.
6. Bake for 15 to 20 minutes, or until a toothpick inserted into the center of a muffin comes out clean.

**Nutritional Information:**

150 Calories - 25g Carbs - 6g Fat - 1g Saturated Fats - 3g Protein - 4g Fibers - 210mg Sodium - 13g Sugar

**Tip:**

- Store in an airtight container to keep them fresh for up to 3 days, or freeze them to have a quick breakfast option on hand.

**Nutritional Benefits:**

- Energy Provision: These muffins provide a balanced amount of carbohydrates to start your day with energy.

# 14. Heart's Delight Veggie Omelette

**Prep Time:** 10 minutes | **Cooking Time:** 10 minutes | **Serving Size:** 2

**Ingredients**

- 1 cup egg whites
- 1/4 cup skim milk
- Salt and black pepper, to taste
- 1/2 cup diced bell peppers
- 1/4 cup diced tomatoes
- 1/4 cup diced onions
- 1/4 cup shredded low-fat cheddar cheese
- 1 tablespoon olive oil

**Instructions**

1. In a medium bowl, whisk together egg whites, skim milk, salt, and black pepper.
2. Heat olive oil in a non-stick skillet over medium heat.
3. Add bell peppers, tomatoes, and onions to the skillet and sauté for 3-4 minutes until they are tender.
4. Pour egg mixture over the vegetables and cook without stirring for about 2-3 minutes, or until the edges start to set.
5. Sprinkle shredded cheddar cheese on top.
6. Gently fold the omelette in half using a spatula, and continue to cook for another 2-3 minutes, or until the cheese is melted and the egg whites are fully cooked.
7. Slide the omelette onto a plate, cut in half, and serve immediately.

**Nutritional Information:**

160 Calories - 8g Carbs - 9g Fat - 2g Saturated Fats - 16g Protein - 1g Fibers - 360mg Sodium - 5g Sugar

**Tip:**

- Customize your omelette by adding your favorite vegetables or some cooked lean meat or poultry for extra protein.

**Nutritional Benefits:**

- Low Calorie: This omelette is a low-calorie option packed with protein and veggies, ideal for a heart-healthy diet.

# 15. Nutrient-Packed Spinach and Feta Wrap

**Prep Time:** 10 minutes | **Cooking Time:** 5 minutes | **Serving Size:** 2 wraps

**Ingredients**

- 2 whole grain or whole wheat tortilla wraps
- 2 cups fresh spinach leaves
- 1/4 cup crumbled feta cheese
- 1/4 cup diced red bell pepper
- 1/4 cup diced tomatoes
- 2 tablespoons diced red onion
- 1 tablespoon olive oil
- Salt and black pepper, to taste

**Instructions**

1. Heat a large non-stick skillet over medium heat with 1 tablespoon of olive oil.
2. Add the spinach leaves and sauté for 2-3 minutes, or until wilted.
3. Stir in the bell pepper, tomatoes, and red onion, and continue to sauté for another 2 minutes.
4. Season with salt and black pepper to taste.
5. Divide the vegetable mixture between the two tortillas.
6. Sprinkle crumbled feta cheese on top of the vegetables.
7. Roll up the tortillas, tucking in the sides as you go, to form a wrap.
8. Place the wraps back in the skillet and cook for an additional 2 minutes on each side, or until they are warm and slightly crisp.
9. Cut each wrap in half diagonally and serve immediately.

**Nutritional Information:**

250 Calories - 30g Carbs - 11g Fat - 3g Saturated Fats - 8g Protein - 5g Fibers - 550mg Sodium - 4g Sugar

**Tip:**

- You can use a variety of other fresh vegetables or even some roasted vegetables based on personal preference.

**Nutritional Benefits:**

- Rich in Vitamins: Spinach is high in iron, calcium, and vitamins A, C, and K1.

# 16. Heartbeat Beetroot Smoothie

**Prep Time:** 10 minutes | **Cooking Time:** 0 minutes | **Serving Size:** 2 servings

**Ingredients**

- 1 medium beetroot, peeled and chopped
- 1 banana, peeled
- 1/2 cup fresh or frozen berries (such as strawberries or blueberries)
- 1/2 cup unsweetened almond milk or any other non-dairy milk
- 1 tablespoon chia seeds
- 1 tablespoon honey or maple syrup (optional)
- Ice cubes (optional)

**Instructions**

1. Place beetroot, banana, berries, almond milk, chia seeds, and sweetener (if using) in a blender.
2. Blend on high speed until smooth and creamy, adding more milk if necessary to reach desired consistency.
3. If using, add ice cubes and blend again until smooth.
4. Pour the smoothie into glasses and serve immediately.

**Nutritional Information:**

140 Calories - 27g Carbs - 3g Fat - 0.5g Saturated Fats - 4g Protein - 7g Fibers - 80mg Sodium - 17g Sugar

**Tip:**

- For a colder, thicker smoothie, use frozen banana slices and berries.

**Nutritional Benefits:**

- Heart Health: Beets are known for their ability to support heart health by improving blood pressure and circulation.

# 17. Breakfast Bars

**Prep Time:** 15 minutes | **Cooking Time:** 20 minutes | **Serving Size:** 12 bars

**Ingredients**

- 2 cups rolled oats
- 1/2 cup almond butter
- 1/4 cup honey or maple syrup
- 1/2 cup unsweetened shredded coconut
- 1/4 cup chopped almonds
- 1/4 cup dried cranberries or cherries
- 2 tablespoons chia seeds
- 1/2 teaspoon cinnamon
- 1/4 teaspoon salt

## Instructions

1. Preheat the oven to 350°F (175°C). Line a baking dish with parchment paper.

2. In a large mixing bowl, combine the rolled oats, almond butter, honey or maple syrup, shredded coconut, chopped almonds, dried cranberries or cherries, chia seeds, cinnamon, and salt.

3. Press the mixture firmly into the prepared baking dish, ensuring it's evenly spread.

4. Bake in the preheated oven for 20-25 minutes or until the edges are golden brown.

5. Allow the bars to cool completely before cutting into 12 bars. Store in an airtight container for up to a week.

**Nutritional** Information:

180 Calories - 20g Carbs - 9g Fat - 1g Saturated Fats - 5g Protein - 4g Fibers - 55mg Sodium - 8g Sugar

**Tip**:

- Substitute almond butter with peanut or cashew butter if preferred.

**Nutritional Benefits:**

- Oats are a great source of soluble fiber which can help lower cholesterol levels.

# 18. Risc and Shine Nut Butter Bowl

**Prep Time:** 10 minutes | **Cooking Time:** 0 minutes | **Serving Size:** 2

## Ingredients

- 2 frozen bananas
- 2 tablespoons almond butter or peanut butter
- 1/4 cup unsweetened almond milk
- 1 tablespoon chia seeds
- 1 tablespoon honey or maple syrup (optional)
- 1/4 cup granola
- 1/4 cup fresh berries (strawberries, blueberries, raspberries)

## Instructions

1. In a high-speed blender, combine the frozen bananas, almond or peanut butter, almond milk, chia seeds, and honey or maple syrup if using.

2. Blend until smooth and creamy, adding more almond milk if necessary to reach desired consistency.

3. Pour into bowls and top with granola and fresh berries.

4. Serve immediately and enjoy a nourishing start to your day!

**Nutritional Information:**

280 Calories - 35g Carbs - 12g Fat - 1.5g Saturated Fats - 8g Protein - 8g Fibers - 55mg Sodium - 18g Sugar

**Tip**:

- Top with additional nuts or seeds for extra protein and crunch.

**Nutritional Benefits:**

- Almond butter provides healthy fats that are beneficial for heart health.

# 19. Heartful Hemp Seed Granola

**Prep Time:** 10 minutes | **Cooking Time:** 25 minutes | **Serving Size:** 10 servings

## Ingredients

- 2 cups old-fashioned rolled oats
- 1/2 cup shelled hemp seeds
- 1/4 cup unsweetened shredded coconut
- 1/4 cup chopped almonds or walnuts
- 1/4 cup honey or maple syrup
- 2 tablespoons coconut oil, melted
- 1/2 teaspoon vanilla extract
- 1/4 teaspoon cinnamon
- 1/4 teaspoon salt

## Instructions

1. Preheat the oven to 300°F (150°C). Line a baking sheet with parchment paper.
2. In a large mixing bowl, combine the rolled oats, hemp seeds, shredded coconut, chopped nuts, honey or maple syrup, melted coconut oil, vanilla extract, cinnamon, and salt.
3. Spread the mixture evenly on the prepared baking sheet.
4. Bake in the preheated oven for 25-30 minutes, stirring halfway through, until the granola is golden brown.
5. Allow the granola to cool completely on the baking sheet before breaking into clusters. Store in an airtight container for up to 2 weeks.

## Nutritional Information:

180 Calories - 20g Carbs - 9g Fat - 2g Saturated Fats - 5g Protein - 4g Fibers - 60mg Sodium - 8g Sugar

## Tip:

- Enjoy with yogurt and fresh fruit for a heart-healthy breakfast.

## Nutritional Benefits:

- Hemp seeds are a great source of omega-3 fatty acids which are beneficial for heart health.

# 20. Savory Breakfast Quiche

**Prep Time:** 15 minutes | **Cooking Time:** 45 minutes | **Serving Size:** 6

## Ingredients

- 1 pre-made whole wheat pie crust
- 6 large egg whites
- 1/4 cup unsweetened almond milk
- 1/2 cup chopped spinach
- 1/2 cup diced tomatoes
- 1/4 cup diced bell peppers
- 1/4 cup shredded mozzarella cheese (optional)
- Salt and black pepper to taste
- 1/4 teaspoon dried basil
- 1/4 teaspoon dried oregano

## Instructions

1. Preheat the oven to 375°F (190°C). Place the pie crust in a 9-inch pie dish and set aside.
2. In a large mixing bowl, whisk together the egg whites, almond milk, salt, black pepper, dried basil, and dried oregano.
3. Stir in the chopped spinach, diced tomatoes, diced bell peppers, and shredded mozzarella cheese if using.
4. Pour the egg mixture into the pie crust and spread out the veggies evenly with a spoon or spatula.
5. Bake in the preheated oven for 45-50 minutes, or until the quiche is set and the top is lightly golden.
6. Allow the quiche to cool for about 10 minutes before slicing and serving. Enjoy warm.

## Nutritional Information:

150 Calories - 15g Carbs - 7g Fat - 2g Saturated Fats - 9g Protein - 2g Fibers - 200mg Sodium - 2g Sugar

## Tip:

- Feel free to use any veggies you have on hand, like mushrooms, onions, or zucchini.

## Nutritional Benefits:

- Spinach is high in nutrients and antioxidants, which can benefit heart health.

# Chapter 5:    Lunch Recipes

## 21. Heartfelt Veggie-Packed Chili

**Prep Time:** 15 minutes | **Cooking Time:** 45 minutes | **Serving Size:** 4-6 servings

**Ingredients**

- 2 tablespoons olive oil
- 1 medium onion, diced
- 3 cloves garlic, minced
- 2 bell peppers, diced
- 2 carrots, diced
- 1 zucchini, diced
- 1 cup mushrooms, chopped
- 2 (15-ounce) cans black beans, drained and rinsed
- 2 (15-ounce) cans kidney beans, drained and rinsed
- 1 (15-ounce) can diced tomatoes, with juices
- 2 cups vegetable broth
- 2 tablespoons chili powder
- 1 tablespoon cumin
- 1 teaspoon paprika
- Salt and pepper, to taste
- Optional toppings: Avocado slices, fresh cilantro, shredded cheese, and a dollop of Greek yogurt

**Instructions**

1. Heat the olive oil in a large pot over medium heat. Add the onion and garlic and sauté for 2-3 minutes until they begin to soften.

2. Add the bell peppers, carrots, zucchini, and mushrooms to the pot and continue sautéing for another 5-7 minutes, until the vegetables are tender.

3. Stir in the black beans, kidney beans, diced tomatoes, vegetable broth, chili powder, cumin, paprika, salt, and pepper.

4. Bring the mixture to a boil, then reduce the heat to low and let it simmer for 30-35 minutes, stirring occasionally.

5. Taste and adjust the seasonings, if necessary.

6. Serve hot, garnished with optional toppings like avocado slices, fresh cilantro, shredded cheese, and a dollop of Greek yogurt.

**Nutritional Information:**

230 calories - 35g carbs - 7g fat - 2g saturated fats - 12g protein - 13g fibers - 580mg sodium - 6g sugar

**Tip:**

- You can use any combination of beans such as pinto beans or white beans based on your preference

**Nutritional Benefits:**

- Rich in plant-based protein which is beneficial for heart health and overall well-being.

# 22. Tender Greens and Grains Bowl

**Prep Time:** 20 minutes | **Cooking Time:** 40 minutes | **Serving Size:** 4 servings

**Ingredients**

- 1 cup quinoa, rinsed and drained
- 2 cups water
- 2 tablespoons olive oil
- 1 cup chickpeas, cooked and drained
- 1/2 teaspoon paprika
- 1/2 teaspoon garlic powder
- Salt and pepper, to taste
- 2 cups mixed greens (spinach, arugula, kale)
- 1/2 cup cherry tomatoes, halved
- 1/4 cup cucumber, sliced
- 1/4 cup red onion, finely diced
- 1/4 cup feta cheese, crumbled
- 1/4 cup Kalamata olives, pitted and halved
- 2 tablespoons balsamic vinaigrette

## Instructions

1. Combine the quinoa and water in a medium saucepan and bring to a boil over high heat. Reduce heat to low, cover, and simmer for 15-20 minutes, or until quinoa is cooked and water is absorbed. Fluff with a fork and set aside.

2. Meanwhile, heat olive oil in a skillet over medium heat. Add chickpeas, paprika, garlic powder, salt, and pepper, and sauté for 5-7 minutes, or until chickpeas are golden and crispy. Remove from heat and set aside.

3. In a large mixing bowl, combine cooked quinoa, crispy chickpeas, mixed greens, cherry tomatoes, cucumber, red onion, feta cheese, and Kalamata olives.

4. Drizzle with balsamic vinaigrette and gently toss to combine all ingredients.

5. Divide the mixture equally among 4 serving bowls and serve immediately, or cover and refrigerate for up to 2 days.

## Nutritional Information:

275 calories - 35g carbs - 12g fat - 3g saturated fats - 9g protein - 7g fibers - 380mg sodium - 5g sugar

## Tip:

- You can substitute quinoa with other grains like farro, barley, or brown rice based on your preference.

## Nutritional Benefits:

- The mixed greens are rich in antioxidants and phytonutrients which are beneficial for heart health.

# 23. Lentil Soup

**Prep Time:** 15 minutes | **Cooking Time:** 45 minutes | **Serving Size:** 4 servings

## Ingredients

- 1 cup green lentils, rinsed and drained
- 4 cups vegetable broth
- 1 tablespoon olive oil
- 1 onion, diced
- 2 carrots, diced
- 2 celery stalks, diced
- 2 garlic cloves, minced
- 1 teaspoon ground cumin
- 1/2 teaspoon turmeric
- Salt and pepper, to taste
- 2 tablespoons fresh parsley, chopped (for garnish)

## Instructions

1. In a large pot, heat olive oil over medium heat. Add onion, carrots, and celery, and sauté for 5-7 minutes until vegetables are softened.

2. Stir in garlic, cumin, and turmeric, and sauté for another minute until fragrant.

3. Add lentils and vegetable broth to the pot, and bring to a boil.

4. Reduce heat to low, cover, and simmer for 35-40 minutes until lentils are tender.

5. Season with salt and pepper to taste. Garnish with fresh parsley before serving.

**Nutritional Information:**

210 calories - 35g carbs - 3g fat - 0.5g saturated fats - 14g protein - 15g fibers - 560mg sodium - 4g sugar

**Tip:**

- For a creamier texture, blend half the soup with an immersion blender.

**Nutritional Benefits:**

- Turmeric contains curcumin, a potent anti-inflammatory compound.

# 24. Cardio-Careful Chickpea Salad

**Prep Time:** 15 minutes | **Cooking Time:** 0 minutes | **Serving Size:** 4 servings

**Ingredients**

- 2 cups chickpeas, cooked and drained
- 1 cup cherry tomatoes, halved
- 1 cucumber, diced
- 1/2 red onion, finely chopped
- 1/4 cup fresh parsley, chopped
- 1/4 cup olive oil
- 2 tablespoons lemon juice
- Salt and pepper, to taste

**Instructions**

1. In a large bowl, combine chickpeas, cherry tomatoes, cucumber, red onion, and parsley.
2. In a small bowl, whisk together olive oil, lemon juice, salt, and pepper.
3. Pour the dressing over the chickpea mixture and toss well to combine.
4. Serve immediately or refrigerate for up to 2 days.

**Nutritional Information:**

260 calories - 30g carbs - 14g fat - 2g saturated fats - 7g protein - 8g fibers - 10mg sodium - 5g sugar

**Tip:**

- You can replace lemon juice with balsamic vinegar for a different flavor profile.

**Nutritional Benefits:**

- Olive oil is a healthy fat that can help reduce inflammation and lower cholesterol levels.

# 25. Wholesome Vegetable Stir-Fry

**Prep Time:** 15 minutes | **Cooking Time:** 15 minutes | **Serving Size:** 4 servings

## Ingredients

- 2 tablespoons olive oil
- 2 bell peppers, sliced
- 1 carrot, julienned
- 1 zucchini, sliced
- 1/2 cup snap peas, halved
- 1/4 cup low-sodium soy sauce
- 2 tablespoons honey
- 1 tablespoon fresh ginger, grated
- 2 garlic cloves, minced
- 1 tablespoon sesame seeds
- 2 green onions, chopped (for garnish)

## Instructions

1. In a large skillet or wok, heat olive oil over medium-high heat. Add bell peppers, carrot, zucchini, and snap peas, and stir-fry for 5-7 minutes until vegetables are tender-crisp.
2. In a small bowl, whisk together soy sauce, honey, ginger, and garlic. Pour over the vegetables and toss well to coat.
3. Cook for another 2-3 minutes until vegetables are glazed.
4. Sprinkle with sesame seeds and garnish with green onions before serving.

## Nutritional Information:

160 calories - 20g carbs - 8g fat - 1g saturated fats - 3g protein - 3g fibers - 580mg sodium - 13g sugar

## Tip:

- For a spicier kick, add a teaspoon of sriracha to the sauce.

## Nutritional Benefits:

- Ginger and garlic have anti-inflammatory properties and can help improve cholesterol levels.

# 26. Olive Heart Mediterranean Wrap

**Prep Time:** 15 minutes | **Cooking Time:** 0 minutes | **Serving Size:** 4 wraps

**Ingredients**

- 4 whole-grain tortilla wraps
- 1 cup hummus
- 1 cucumber, sliced
- 1 red bell pepper, sliced
- 1/2 cup Kalamata olives, pitted and sliced
- 1/2 cup feta cheese, crumbled
- 1/4 cup red onion, thinly sliced
- 1/4 cup fresh parsley, chopped

**Instructions**

1. Lay out the tortilla wraps on a clean surface.
2. Spread a quarter cup of hummus on each wrap.
3. Arrange cucumber, red bell pepper, olives, feta cheese, red onion, and parsley evenly among the wraps.
4. Roll up the wraps tightly, tucking in the sides as you go. Cut each wrap in half diagonally before serving.

**Nutritional Information:**

320 calories - 40g carbs - 16g fat - 4g saturated fats - 12g protein - 7g fibers - 720mg sodium - 5g sugar

**Tip:**

- Use whole-grain or gluten-free wraps to suit your dietary needs.

**Nutritional Benefits:**

- Hummus provides protein and essential nutrients while being low in saturated fat.

# 27. Harmony Quinoa Salad

**Prep Time:** 15 minutes | **Cooking Time:** 20 minutes | **Serving Size:** 4 servings

## Ingredients

- 1 cup quinoa, rinsed and drained
- 2 cups water
- 1/2 cup cherry tomatoes, halved
- 1/2 cup cucumber, diced
- 1/4 cup red onion, finely diced
- 1/4 cup fresh parsley, chopped
- 1/4 cup fresh mint, chopped
- 2 tablespoons olive oil
- 2 tablespoons lemon juice
- Salt and pepper, to taste

## Instructions

1. In a medium saucepan, bring water to a boil. Stir in quinoa, reduce heat to low, cover, and simmer for 15-20 minutes until quinoa is cooked and water is absorbed.
2. Remove from heat and let it cool to room temperature.
3. In a large bowl, combine cooked quinoa, cherry tomatoes, cucumber, red onion, parsley, and mint.
4. In a small bowl, whisk together olive oil, lemon juice, salt, and pepper. Pour dressing over quinoa mixture and toss well to combine.
5. Serve chilled or at room temperature.

## Nutritional Information:

220 calories - 30g carbs - 10g fat - 1.5g saturated fats - 6g protein - 4g fibers - 10mg sodium - 2g sugar

## Tip:

- This salad can be made ahead and refrigerated for up to 2 days.

## Nutritional Benefits:

- Quinoa is a complete protein and a great source of fiber, supporting heart health and digestion.

# 28. Soulful Minestrone

**Prep Time:** 20 minutes | **Cooking Time:** 40 minutes | **Serving Size:** 6 servings

## Ingredients

- 2 tablespoons olive oil
- 1 onion, diced
- 2 carrots, diced
- 2 celery stalks, diced
- 3 garlic cloves, minced
- 1 zucchini, diced
- 1 cup green beans, cut into 1-inch pieces
- 4 cups low-sodium vegetable broth
- 2 cups water
- 1 can (15 oz) low-sodium diced tomatoes
- 1 can (15 oz) kidney beans, rinsed and drained
- 1/2 cup small pasta (like ditalini or small shells)
- 1/2 teaspoon dried oregano
- 1/2 teaspoon dried basil
- Salt and pepper, to taste
- 1/4 cup fresh parsley, chopped (for garnish)

## Instructions

1. In a large pot, heat olive oil over medium heat. Add onion, carrots, and celery, and sauté for 5-7 minutes until vegetables are softened.
2. Stir in garlic, zucchini, and green beans, and sauté for another 3-4 minutes.
3. Add vegetable broth, water, diced tomatoes, kidney beans, pasta, oregano, and basil to the pot. Bring to a boil.
4. Reduce heat to low, cover, and simmer for 25-30 minutes until vegetables and pasta are tender.
1. Season with salt and pepper to taste. Garnish with fresh parsley before serving.

## Nutritional Information:

210 calories - 35g carbs - 5g fat - 1g saturated fats - 8g protein - 9g fibers - 430mg sodium - 7g sugar

## Tip:

- This soup is perfect for meal prep and freezes well.

## Nutritional Benefits:

- Kidney beans are a great source of protein and fiber, which are essential for heart health.

# 29. Loving Pita Pockets

**Prep Time:** 15 minutes | **Cooking Time:** 0 minutes | **Serving Size:** 4 pita pockets

**Ingredients**

- 4 whole-grain pita pockets
- 1 can (15 oz) chickpeas, rinsed and drained
- 1/2 cup cucumber, diced
- 1/2 cup cherry tomatoes, halved
- 1/4 cup red onion, finely diced
- 1/4 cup fresh parsley, chopped
- 2 tablespoons olive oil
- 2 tablespoons lemon juice
- Salt and pepper, to taste

**Instructions**

1. In a large bowl, combine chickpeas, cucumber, cherry tomatoes, red onion, and parsley.
2. Drizzle olive oil and lemon juice over the chickpea mixture, and toss well to combine. Season with salt and pepper to taste.
3. Cut the pita pockets in half and open each half to form a pocket.
4. Fill each pita pocket with the chickpea salad mixture.
5. Serve immediately or refrigerate for later use.

**Nutritional Information:**

280 calories - 45g carbs - 9g fat - 1.2g saturated fats - 10g protein - 9g fibers - 290mg sodium - 6g sugar

**Tip:**

- Experiment with different herbs like mint or dill for a new flavor profile.

**Nutritional Benefits:**

- Chickpeas are a great source of protein and fiber, supporting heart health and digestion

# 30. Nourishing Nicoise Salad

**Prep Time:** 20 minutes | **Cooking Time:** 10 minutes | **Serving Size:** 4 servings

**Ingredients**

- 4 cups mixed salad greens
- 2 cans (5 oz each) no-salt-added tuna in water, drained
- 12 small new potatoes, cooked and halved
- 1 cup green beans, cooked and halved
- 1/2 cup Kalamata olives, pitted and halved
- 4 hard-boiled eggs, quartered

- 2 tomatoes, cut into wedges
- 1/4 cup red wine vinegar
- 1/4 cup extra-virgin olive oil
- 1 teaspoon Dijon mustard
- Salt and pepper, to taste

**Instructions**

1. Arrange the salad greens on a large serving platter or divide among 4 individual plates.
2. Arrange the tuna, potatoes, green beans, olives, eggs, and tomatoes on top of the greens.
3. In a small bowl, whisk together red wine vinegar, olive oil, Dijon mustard, salt, and pepper until well combined.
4. Drizzle the dressing over the salad before serving.

**Nutritional Information:**

350 calories - 30g carbs - 18g fat - 3g saturated fats - 20g protein - 6g fibers - 530mg sodium - 6g sugar

**Tip:**

- Use fresh grilled tuna steaks instead of canned tuna for a gourmet touch.

**Nutritional Benefits:**

- Tuna is a rich source of omega-3 fatty acids which are known to improve heart health.

# 31. Vibrant Veggie and Hummus Wrap

**Prep Time:** 15 minutes | **Cooking Time:** 0 minutes | **Serving Size:** 4 wraps

**Ingredients**

- 4 whole-grain tortilla wraps
- 1 cup hummus
- 1 red bell pepper, sliced
- 1 carrot, julienned
- 1 cucumber, julienned
- 1/2 cup red cabbage, shredded
- 1/2 cup fresh spinach leaves
- 1/4 cup fresh mint leaves

**Instructions**

1. Lay out the tortilla wraps on a clean surface.
2. Spread a quarter cup of hummus on each wrap.
3. Arrange red bell pepper, carrot, cucumber, red cabbage, spinach, and mint leaves evenly among the wraps.
4. Roll up the wraps tightly, tucking in the sides as you go. Cut each wrap in half diagonally before serving.

**Nutritional Information:**

290 calories - 40g carbs - 12g fat - 2g saturated fats - 10g protein - 9g fibers - 540mg sodium - 5g sugar

**Tip:**

- Add grilled chicken strips or tofu for added protein.

**Nutritional Benefits:**

- A variety of colorful vegetables provide essential vitamins, minerals, and antioxidants beneficial for heart health.

## 32. Edamame Bowl

**Prep Time:** 10 minutes | **Cooking Time:** 10 minutes | **Serving Size:** 4 bowls

**Ingredients**

- 2 cups edamame, shelled and cooked
- 1 cup quinoa, cooked
- 1 cup shredded carrots
- 1 cup red cabbage, shredded
- 1/2 cup red bell pepper, thinly sliced
- 1/4 cup green onions, chopped
- 1/4 cup fresh cilantro, chopped
- 2 tablespoons sesame oil
- 2 tablespoons soy sauce, low sodium
- 1 tablespoon rice vinegar
- 1 tablespoon sesame seeds

**Instructions**

1. In a large mixing bowl, combine edamame, quinoa, carrots, red cabbage, red bell pepper, green onions, and cilantro.
2. In a small bowl, whisk together sesame oil, soy sauce, and rice vinegar.
3. Pour the dressing over the edamame mixture and toss well to combine.
4. Divide the mixture among 4 bowls, and sprinkle with sesame seeds before serving.

**Nutritional Information:**

270 calories - 30g carbs - 12g fat - 2g saturated fats - 12g protein - 8g fibers - 400mg sodium - 6g sugar

**Tip:**

- This bowl can be prepared ahead and refrigerated, making it a great option for meal prep.

**Nutritional Benefits:**

- Edamame and quinoa are excellent sources of plant-based protein and fiber which are beneficial for heart health.

# 33. Lemon Herb Chicken Salad

**Prep Time:** 15 minutes | **Cooking Time:** 15 minutes | **Serving Size:** 4 servings

## Ingredients

- 2 boneless, skinless chicken breasts
- 2 tablespoons olive oil
- 1 lemon, zest and juice
- 2 garlic cloves, minced
- 1 teaspoon dried oregano
- Salt and black pepper, to taste
- 6 cups mixed salad greens
- 1/2 cup cherry tomatoes, halved
- 1/4 cup Kalamata olives, pitted and halved
- 1/4 cup red onion, thinly sliced
- 1/4 cup feta cheese, crumbled

## Instructions

1. In a medium bowl, whisk together olive oil, lemon zest, lemon juice, garlic, oregano, salt, and black pepper.
2. Add chicken breasts to the marinade and let sit for at least 30 minutes, or refrigerate overnight.
3. Heat a grill or grill pan over medium-high heat. Cook the chicken for 6-7 minutes on each side or until internal temperature reaches 165°F.
4. Let the chicken rest for a few minutes before slicing.
5. In a large bowl, toss together salad greens, cherry tomatoes, olives, and red onion.
6. Divide the salad among 4 plates, top with sliced chicken and crumbled feta cheese.

## Nutritional Information:

260 calories - 8g carbs - 16g fat - 4g saturated fats - 24g protein - 2g fibers - 320mg sodium - 3g sugar

## Tip:

- Substitute grilled salmon or tofu for chicken for a different protein option.

## Nutritional Benefits:

- Olive oil and olives provide healthy monounsaturated fats which are beneficial for heart health.

# 34. Black Bean Soup

**Prep Time:** 10 minutes | **Cooking Time:** 20 minutes | **Serving Size:** 4 servings

## Ingredients

- 2 cans (15 oz each) black beans, rinsed and drained
- 2 cups vegetable broth, low sodium
- 1 cup onion, diced
- 1/2 cup carrots, diced
- 1/2 cup celery, diced
- 2 garlic cloves, minced
- 1 teaspoon ground cumin
- 1/2 teaspoon chili powder
- Salt and black pepper, to taste
- 1/4 cup fresh cilantro, chopped for garnish
- 1/4 cup plain Greek yogurt, for garnish

## Instructions

1. In a large pot, heat olive oil over medium heat. Add onion, carrots, and celery, and sauté for 5-7 minutes or until vegetables are softened.
2. Stir in garlic, cumin, and chili powder, and cook for an additional minute.
3. Add black beans and vegetable broth to the pot, and bring to a boil.
4. Reduce heat and simmer for 10-15 minutes.
5. Use an immersion blender to partially puree the soup, leaving some texture. Or, carefully transfer half of the soup to a blender, puree, and return to the pot.
6. Season with salt and black pepper to taste.
7. Serve hot, garnished with fresh cilantro and a dollop of Greek yogurt.

## Nutritional Information:

210 calories - 36g carbs - 1g fat - 0g saturated fats - 13g protein - 14g fibers - 300mg sodium - 3g sugar

## Tip:

- This soup can be made in advance and reheated, making it a great meal prep option.

## Nutritional Benefits:

- The high fiber content in black beans helps to lower cholesterol levels and stabilize blood sugar.

# 35. Tender Tofu Stir Fry

**Prep Time:** 15 minutes | **Cooking Time:** 15 minutes | **Serving Size:** 4 servings

## Ingredients

- 1 block (14 oz) firm tofu, pressed and cubed
- 2 tablespoons olive oil
- 2 cups broccoli florets
- 1 red bell pepper, sliced
- 1 carrot, julienned
- 2 green onions, sliced
- 3 tablespoons low-sodium soy sauce
- 1 tablespoon ginger, minced
- 1 tablespoon garlic, minced
- 1 tablespoon cornstarch
- 1/4 cup water
- Sesame seeds, for garnish

## Instructions

1. Heat olive oil in a large skillet or wok over medium-high heat. Add tofu cubes and cook until golden brown on all sides, about 8-10 minutes. Remove tofu from skillet and set aside.
2. In the same skillet, add broccoli, bell pepper, and carrot. Stir-fry for 5-7 minutes or until vegetables are tender-crisp.
3. In a small bowl, whisk together soy sauce, ginger, garlic, cornstarch, and water. Pour the sauce over the vegetables and stir well to coat.
4. Return tofu to the skillet and toss everything together until evenly coated with sauce and heated through.
5. Divide among 4 plates, garnish with green onions and sesame seeds, and serve immediately.

## Nutritional Information:

210 calories - 14g carbs - 12g fat - 2g saturated fats - 14g protein - 4g fibers - 510mg sodium - 5g sugar

## Tip:

- Feel free to add more vegetables or switch them out based on personal preferences.

## Nutritional Benefits:

- Tofu is a good source of protein and contains all nine essential amino acids. It's also an excellent source of iron and calcium.

## 36. Heart-Wise Walnut Salad

**Prep Time:** 10 minutes | **Cooking Time:** 0 minutes | **Serving Size:** 4 servings

**Ingredients**

- 6 cups mixed salad greens
- 1/2 cup walnuts, chopped
- 1/4 cup dried cranberries
- 1/4 cup goat cheese, crumbled
- 1/4 cup balsamic vinaigrette

**Instructions**

1. In a large salad bowl, combine mixed greens, walnuts, dried cranberries, and goat cheese.
2. Drizzle balsamic vinaigrette over the salad and toss gently to combine.
3. Divide salad among 4 plates and serve immediately.

**Nutritional Information:**

230 calories - 15g carbs - 18g fat - 4g saturated fats - 6g protein - 3g fibers - 150mg sodium - 10g sugar

**Tip:**

- Toasting the walnuts beforehand can enhance their flavor and crunch.

**Nutritional Benefits:**

- Walnuts are rich in omega-3 fatty acids, which are known to be heart-healthy.

## 37. Cardio-Care Cauliflower Rice Bowl

**Prep Time:** 10 minutes | **Cooking Time:** 10 minutes | **Serving Size:** 4 servings

**Ingredients**

- 4 cups cauliflower rice
- 2 tablespoons olive oil
- 1/2 cup red bell pepper, diced
- 1/2 cup yellow bell pepper, diced
- 1/2 cup zucchini, diced
- 1/4 cup red onion, diced
- 2 tablespoons fresh cilantro, chopped
- 1/4 cup feta cheese, crumbled
- Salt and black pepper, to taste

**Instructions**

1. Heat olive oil in a large skillet over medium heat. Add cauliflower rice and cook for 5-7 minutes or until tender.
2. Stir in red and yellow bell peppers, zucchini, and red onion, and continue cooking for an additional 5 minutes or until vegetables are tender.
3. Remove from heat, and stir in fresh cilantro, feta cheese, salt, and black pepper.

4. Divide among 4 bowls and serve immediately.

**Nutritional Information:**

160 calories - 12g carbs - 11g fat - 3g saturated fats - 5g protein - 4g fibers - 220mg sodium - 6g sugar

**Tip:**

- Add grilled chicken, shrimp, or tofu for added protein.

**Nutritional Benefits:**

- Cauliflower is a low-calorie vegetable that's high in fiber and vitamin C, which is beneficial for heart health.

# 38. Harmonious Vegetable Soup

**Prep Time:** 15 minutes | **Cooking Time:** 25 minutes | **Serving Size:** 4 servings

**Ingredients**

- 2 tablespoons olive oil
- 1 onion, diced
- 2 carrots, sliced
- 2 celery stalks, chopped
- 3 cloves garlic, minced
- 4 cups low-sodium vegetable broth
- 1 cup diced tomatoes
- 1 cup green beans, cut into 1-inch pieces
- 1/2 cup corn kernels
- 1/2 cup peas
- Salt and black pepper, to taste
- 2 tablespoons fresh parsley, chopped

**Instructions**

1. Heat olive oil in a large pot over medium heat. Add onion, carrots, and celery, and sauté for 5 minutes until vegetables are softened.
2. Stir in garlic and cook for an additional minute.
3. Add vegetable broth, diced tomatoes, green beans, corn, and peas to the pot. Bring to a boil.
4. Reduce heat and let simmer for 15-20 minutes until vegetables are tender.
5. Season with salt and black pepper to taste. Stir in fresh parsley before serving.
6. Divide among 4 bowls and serve hot.

**Nutritional Information:**

140 calories - 23g carbs - 5g fat - 1g saturated fats - 3g protein - 6g fibers - 290mg sodium - 9g sugar

**Tip:**

- For added protein, consider adding beans or lentils.

**Nutritional Benefits:**

- This soup is loaded with various vegetables providing a good source of dietary fiber, vitamins, and minerals that are heart-healthy.

# 39. Roasted Veggie Bowl

**Prep Time:** 15 minutes | **Cooking Time:** 25 minutes | **Serving Size:** 4 servings

## Ingredients

- 2 cups broccoli florets
- 2 cups cauliflower florets
- 2 carrots, sliced
- 1 red bell pepper, chopped
- 1 yellow bell pepper, chopped
- 2 tablespoons olive oil
- Salt and black pepper, to taste
- 1 teaspoon Italian seasoning
- 1/2 cup quinoa, uncooked
- 1/4 cup feta cheese, crumbled
- 2 tablespoons balsamic glaze

## Instructions

1. Preheat oven to 425°F. Toss broccoli, cauliflower, carrots, and bell peppers with olive oil, salt, black pepper, and Italian seasoning on a large baking sheet.
2. Spread vegetables in an even layer and roast for 20-25 minutes, stirring halfway through, until tender and slightly caramelized.
3. While vegetables are roasting, cook quinoa according to package instructions.
4. Divide quinoa among 4 bowls. Top with roasted vegetables, feta cheese, and drizzle with balsamic glaze before serving.

## Nutritional Information:

260 calories - 32g carbs - 11g fat - 3g saturated fats - 8g protein - 6g fibers - 200mg sodium - 10g sugar

## Tip:

- For a vegan option, omit feta cheese or replace with a vegan alternative.

## Nutritional Benefits:

- Quinoa is a good source of protein and is high in fiber which is beneficial for heart health.

# 40. Lentil and Vegetable Stew

**Prep Time:** 10 minutes | **Cooking Time:** 40 minutes | **Serving Size:** 4 servings

## Ingredients

- 2 tablespoons olive oil
- 1 onion, diced
- 2 carrots, diced
- 2 celery stalks, diced
- 3 cloves garlic, minced
- 1 cup green lentils, rinsed and drained
- 4 cups low-sodium vegetable broth
- 1 cup diced tomatoes
- 1 teaspoon cumin
- 1/2 teaspoon coriander
- Salt and black pepper, to taste
- 2 cups spinach, roughly chopped
- Fresh parsley, for garnish

## Instructions

1. Heat olive oil in a large pot over medium heat. Add onion, carrots, and celery, and sauté for 5 minutes until softened.
2. Stir in garlic and cook for an additional minute.
3. Add lentils, vegetable broth, diced tomatoes, cumin, coriander, salt, and black pepper to the pot. Bring to a boil.
4. Reduce heat, cover, and let simmer for 30-35 minutes until lentils are tender.
5. Stir in spinach and cook for an additional 5 minutes.
6. Garnish with fresh parsley before serving. Divide among 4 bowls and serve hot.

## Nutritional Information:

240 calories - 37g carbs - 6g fat - 1g saturated fats - 13g protein - 16g fibers - 290mg sodium - 7g sugar

## Tip:

- For a spicier stew, add a pinch of red pepper flakes.

## Nutritional Benefits:

- Spinach is rich in vitamins A, C, and K, and is a good source of magnesium, iron, and folate.

# Chapter 6:    Dinner Recipes

## 41. Baked Salmon

**Prep Time:** 10 minutes | **Cooking Time:** 20 minutes | **Serving Size:** 4

**Ingredients**

- 4 salmon fillets
- 2 tablespoons olive oil
- 1 teaspoon garlic powder
- 1 teaspoon onion powder
- 1/2 teaspoon paprika
- Salt and pepper to taste
- 2 tablespoons fresh lemon juice
- 2 tablespoons fresh dill, finely chopped
- Lemon slices for garnish

**Instructions**

1. Preheat the oven to 400°F (200°C). Line a baking sheet with parchment paper.
2. In a small bowl, mix together the olive oil, garlic powder, onion powder, paprika, salt, and pepper.
3. Place the salmon fillets on the prepared baking sheet. Brush the mixture over the salmon fillets evenly.
4. Drizzle lemon juice over the salmon fillets and sprinkle with fresh dill.
5. Bake in the preheated oven for about 15-20 minutes, or until the salmon flakes easily with a fork.
6. Garnish with additional lemon slices and dill if desired, and serve immediately.

**Nutritional Information:**

258 Calories - 2g Carbs - 14g Fat - 2g Saturated Fats - 29g Protein - 0g Fibers - 67mg Sodium - 1g Sugar

**Tip:**

- For a crispier crust, you can broil the salmon for an additional 2-3 minutes before serving.

**Nutritional Benefits:**

- Rich in Omega-3 fatty acids which are known to reduce heart disease risk factors.

# 42. Tender Heart Turkey Meatballs

**Prep Time:** 15 minutes | **Cooking Time:** 25 minutes | **Serving Size:** 4

## Ingredients

- 1 lb ground turkey
- 1/4 cup whole wheat breadcrumbs
- 1/4 cup grated Parmesan cheese
- 1/4 cup fresh parsley, finely chopped
- 2 cloves garlic, minced
- 1 large egg
- Salt and pepper to taste
- 1 tablespoon olive oil
- 2 cups low-sodium marinara sauce
- Fresh basil for garnish (optional)

## Instructions

1. In a large mixing bowl, combine ground turkey, breadcrumbs, Parmesan cheese, parsley, garlic, egg, salt, and pepper. Mix until well combined but do not overmix to keep the meatballs tender.
2. Shape the mixture into 16 meatballs, approximately 1-inch in diameter.
3. Heat olive oil in a large skillet over medium heat. Once hot, add the meatballs and cook for 6-8 minutes, turning occasionally, until browned on all sides.
4. Pour marinara sauce over the meatballs, cover, and simmer for about 15-20 minutes until the meatballs are cooked through.
5. Garnish with fresh basil if desired and serve hot, perhaps over whole grain spaghetti or zucchini noodles.

## Nutritional Information:

266 Calories - 9g Carbs - 15g Fat - 4g Saturated Fats - 24g Protein - 2g Fibers - 520mg Sodium - 4g Sugar

## Tip:

- Substitute ground turkey with ground chicken or lean ground beef if desired.

## Nutritional Benefits:

- Lean turkey provides a lower-fat source of protein which is heart-friendly.

# 43. Stuffed Peppers

**Prep Time:** 20 minutes | **Cooking Time:** 35 minutes | **Serving Size:** 4

## Ingredients

- 4 large bell peppers, halved and seeds removed
- 1 cup quinoa, cooked
- 1 cup black beans, cooked and drained
- 1 cup corn kernels, fresh or frozen
- 1 teaspoon olive oil
- 1/2 cup onion, finely chopped
- 2 cloves garlic, minced
- 1 teaspoon cumin
- 1/2 teaspoon chili powder
- Salt and pepper to taste
- 1 cup low-sodium tomato sauce
- 1/4 cup shredded low-fat cheddar cheese (optional)
- Fresh parsley or cilantro for garnish

## Instructions

1. Preheat the oven to 375°F (190°C).
2. In a large skillet, heat olive oil over medium heat. Add onion and garlic, sautéing until translucent.
3. Stir in cumin, chili powder, black beans, corn, and cooked quinoa. Season with salt and pepper to taste. Cook for another 2-3 minutes.
4. Place bell pepper halves in a baking dish and fill each with the quinoa mixture.
5. Pour tomato sauce over the stuffed peppers. Cover with aluminum foil.
6. Bake in the preheated oven for 30-35 minutes, or until the peppers are tender.
7. If using cheese, sprinkle over the top of each pepper and return to the oven for an additional 5 minutes, or until the cheese is melted.
8. Garnish with fresh parsley or cilantro before serving.

## Nutritional Information:

225 Calories - 40g Carbs - 3g Fat - 1g Saturated Fats - 9g Protein - 9g Fibers - 290mg Sodium - 11g Sugar

## Tip:

- Substitute quinoa with brown rice or farro for variety.

## Nutritional Benefits:

- High in dietary fiber which supports heart health by helping to lower cholesterol.

# 44. Vegetable Stew

**Prep Time:** 15 minutes | **Cooking Time:** 40 minutes | **Serving Size:** 6

## Ingredients

- 1 tablespoon olive oil
- 1 onion, diced
- 2 carrots, sliced
- 2 stalks celery, chopped
- 3 cloves garlic, minced
- 1 zucchini, chopped
- 1 sweet potato, peeled and diced
- 4 cups low-sodium vegetable broth
- 1 (14.5 oz) can diced tomatoes, undrained
- 1 teaspoon thyme
- 1/2 teaspoon rosemary
- Salt and pepper to taste
- 2 cups kale, chopped
- 1 (15 oz) can white beans, drained and rinsed

## Instructions

1. Heat olive oil in a large pot over medium heat. Add onion, carrots, and celery, sautéing for about 5-7 minutes until vegetables are softened.
2. Stir in garlic, zucchini, and sweet potato, and continue to cook for another 3-4 minutes.
3. Add vegetable broth, diced tomatoes with their juice, thyme, rosemary, salt, and pepper. Bring to a boil.
4. Reduce heat, cover, and simmer for about 25-30 minutes, or until the vegetables are tender.
5. Stir in kale and white beans, cooking for another 5-7 minutes until kale is wilted and beans are heated through.
6. Adjust seasoning if necessary, and serve hot, garnished with fresh herbs if desired.

## Nutritional Information:

160 Calories - 30g Carbs - 2g Fat - 0g Saturated Fats - 7g Protein - 8g Fibers - 420mg Sodium - 7g Sugar

## Tip:

- For a heartier stew, add cooked chicken or turkey.

## Nutritional Benefits:

- Packed with various vegetables providing a range of antioxidants beneficial for heart health.

# 45. Lemon-Herb Chicken

**Prep Time:** 15 minutes | **Cooking Time:** 25 minutes | **Serving Size:** 4

## Ingredients

- 4 boneless, skinless chicken breasts
- 2 tablespoons olive oil
- Zest and juice of 1 lemon
- 2 cloves garlic, minced
- 1 teaspoon dried oregano
- 1/2 teaspoon dried thyme
- 1/2 teaspoon dried rosemary
- Salt and black pepper to taste
- Fresh parsley for garnish

## Instructions

1. In a medium bowl, mix together the olive oil, lemon zest, lemon juice, garlic, oregano, thyme, rosemary, salt, and black pepper.
2. Place the chicken breasts in a shallow dish and pour the marinade over them. Cover and let marinate in the refrigerator for at least 30 minutes, or up to 2 hours.
3. Preheat the grill or stovetop grill pan over medium-high heat.
4. Remove the chicken from the marinade and discard the marinade. Place the chicken on the grill and cook for about 6-7 minutes per side, or until the internal temperature reaches 165°F (75°C) and the chicken is no longer pink in the center.
5. Remove from the grill and let rest for a few minutes before serving. Garnish with fresh parsley.

## Nutritional Information:

220 Calories - 2g Carbs - 11g Fat - 2g Saturated Fats - 28g Protein - 0g Fibers - 70mg Sodium - 1g Sugar

## Tip:

- Pair with a side of steamed vegetables and quinoa for a balanced meal.

## Nutritional Benefits:

- Lean source of protein which is crucial for heart health.

# 46. Grilled Veggies Platter

**Prep Time:** 20 minutes | **Cooking Time:** 15 minutes | **Serving Size:** 4

## Ingredients

- 2 bell peppers, sliced
- 2 zucchinis, sliced lengthwise
- 2 yellow squashes, sliced lengthwise
- 1 red onion, cut into wedges
- 1 tablespoon olive oil
- Salt and black pepper to taste
- 2 tablespoons balsamic glaze
- Fresh parsley or basil for garnish

## Instructions

1. Preheat the grill to medium-high heat.
2. Toss the vegetables with olive oil, salt, and pepper.
3. Place the vegetables on the grill and cook for about 3-5 minutes per side, until they are tender and have grill marks.
4. Remove the vegetables from the grill and arrange them on a platter.
5. Drizzle with balsamic glaze and garnish with fresh parsley or basil before serving.

## Nutritional Information:

90 Calories - 16g Carbs - 4g Fat - 0.5g Saturated Fats - 3g Protein - 4g Fibers - 10mg Sodium - 10g Sugar

## Tip:

- Serve alongside grilled chicken, fish, or a hearty grain salad for a complete meal.

## Nutritional Benefits:

- Provides a low-calorie, nutrient-dense side dish option.

# 47. Tender Touch Tofu Stir-Fry

**Prep Time:** 15 minutes | **Cooking Time:** 20 minutes | **Serving Size:** 4

## Ingredients

- 1 (14-ounce) block extra-firm tofu, drained and cubed
- 2 tablespoons olive oil, divided
- 2 cups broccoli florets
- 1 red bell pepper, sliced
- 1 carrot, julienned
- 2 cloves garlic, minced
- 1/4 cup low-sodium soy sauce
- 1 tablespoon cornstarch
- 1 tablespoon water
- 1 tablespoon maple syrup or honey
- 1 teaspoon sesame oil
- 2 green onions, sliced for garnish
- Sesame seeds for garnish

## Instructions

1. Press the tofu between paper towels to remove excess moisture, then cut into cubes.
2. Heat 1 tablespoon olive oil in a large skillet or wok over medium-high heat. Add the tofu and cook until golden brown on all sides, about 8-10 minutes. Remove tofu from skillet and set aside.
3. In the same skillet, add the remaining 1 tablespoon olive oil. Stir in broccoli, bell pepper, and carrot, and stir-fry for about 5-7 minutes, until vegetables are tender-crisp.
4. In a small bowl, whisk together the soy sauce, cornstarch, water, maple syrup or honey, and sesame oil to make the sauce.
5. Add the tofu back to the skillet, pour the sauce over the tofu and vegetables, and stir well to combine. Cook for another 2-3 minutes, until everything is heated through.
6. Garnish with green onions and sesame seeds before serving.

## Nutritional Information:

210 Calories - 16g Carbs - 12g Fat - 2g Saturated Fats - 14g Protein - 4g Fibers - 550mg Sodium - 6g Sugar

## Tip:

- Substitute tofu with chicken or shrimp for a non-vegetarian option.

## Nutritional Benefits:

- Tofu is a good source of plant-based protein and contains all nine essential amino acids.

# 48. Heartfelt Herb-Crusted Tilapia

**Prep Time:** 10 minutes | **Cooking Time:** 10 minutes | **Serving Size:** 4

## Ingredients

- 4 tilapia fillets
- 2 tablespoons olive oil
- 1/2 cup whole wheat bread crumbs
- 1 teaspoon dried parsley
- 1 teaspoon dried oregano
- 1/2 teaspoon garlic powder
- 1/4 teaspoon black pepper
- 1/4 teaspoon salt
- Lemon wedges for serving

## Instructions

1. Preheat the oven to 425°F (220°C) and lightly grease a baking sheet.
2. In a shallow bowl, mix together the bread crumbs, parsley, oregano, garlic powder, black pepper, and salt.
3. Brush both sides of the tilapia fillets with olive oil, then press into the herb and breadcrumb mixture to coat.
4. Place the coated fillets on the prepared baking sheet.
5. Bake for 10 minutes, or until the fish flakes easily with a fork.
6. Serve hot with lemon wedges on the side.

## Nutritional Information:

190 Calories - 5g Carbs - 9g Fat - 1.5g Saturated Fats - 24g Protein - 0g Fibers - 160mg Sodium - 0g Sugar

## Tip:

- Substitute tilapia with other white fish like cod or haddock if desired.

## Nutritional Benefits:

- Tilapia is a lean source of protein which is essential for heart health.

# 49. Nourish Heart Veggie Spaghetti

**Prep Time:** 20 minutes | **Cooking Time:** 20 minutes | **Serving Size:** 4

## Ingredients

- 8 ounces whole-grain spaghetti
- 2 tablespoons olive oil
- 2 cloves garlic, minced
- 1 bell pepper, thinly sliced
- 1 carrot, julienned
- 1 zucchini, julienned
- 2 tomatoes, diced
- Salt and black pepper to taste
- Fresh basil or parsley for garnish
- Grated Parmesan cheese (optional)

## Instructions

1. Cook the spaghetti according to the package instructions, then drain and set aside.
2. In a large skillet, heat the olive oil over medium heat. Add the garlic and cook for 1 minute.
3. Add the bell pepper, carrot, and zucchini to the skillet, and sauté for about 5-7 minutes, or until the vegetables are tender.
4. Stir in the tomatoes, salt, and black pepper, and cook for an additional 2-3 minutes, or until the tomatoes are soft.
5. Toss the cooked spaghetti with the vegetable mixture.
6. Garnish with fresh basil or parsley, and grated Parmesan cheese if desired, before serving.

## Nutritional Information:

250 Calories - 35g Carbs - 9g Fat - 1.5g Saturated Fats - 8g Protein - 6g Fibers - 10mg Sodium - 5g Sugar

## Tip:

- Use a vegetable spiralizer to create veggie noodles for a low-carb option.

## Nutritional Benefits:

- Rich in colorful vegetables providing a variety of antioxidants and nutrients.

## 50. Heart's Embrace Eggplant Casserole

**Prep Time:** 20 minutes | **Cooking Time:** 45 minutes | **Serving Size:** 6

### Ingredients

- 2 large eggplants, sliced into 1/2-inch rounds
- Olive oil spray
- Salt and black pepper to taste
- 2 cups marinara sauce (low-sodium)
- 2 cups shredded mozzarella cheese (part-skim)
- 1/4 cup grated Parmesan cheese
- 1/2 teaspoon dried basil
- 1/2 teaspoon dried oregano
- Fresh basil or parsley for garnish

### Instructions

1. Preheat the oven to 375°F (190°C).
2. Arrange the eggplant slices in a single layer on baking sheets and lightly spray both sides with olive oil spray. Season with salt and black pepper.
3. Bake for 15 minutes, flipping halfway through, until the eggplant is tender and slightly golden.
4. In a baking dish, spread a thin layer of marinara sauce. Layer half of the eggplant slices over the sauce, then top with half of the mozzarella and Parmesan cheeses. Sprinkle with half of the basil and oregano.
5. Repeat layers with remaining ingredients.
6. Bake for 30 minutes, or until the cheese is bubbly and golden brown.
7. Garnish with fresh basil or parsley before serving.

### Nutritional Information:

160 Calories - 15g Carbs - 8g Fat - 4g Saturated Fats - 11g Protein - 5g Fibers - 450mg Sodium - 8g Sugar

### Tip:

- Serve with a side salad to increase your vegetable intake.

### Nutritional Benefits:

- Cheese provides calcium which is important for bone health, but in moderation due to its saturated fat content.

# 51. Walnut Pesto Pasta

**Prep Time:** 10 minutes | **Cooking Time:** 12 minutes | **Serving Size:** 4

## Ingredients

- 8 ounces whole-grain spaghetti
- 1 cup fresh basil leaves
- 1/2 cup walnuts
- 2 cloves garlic
- 1/4 cup grated Parmesan cheese
- 1/4 cup extra virgin olive oil
- Salt and black pepper to taste
- Cherry tomatoes and extra walnuts for garnish (optional)

## Instructions

1. Cook the spaghetti according to the package instructions until al dente, then drain and set aside.
2. In a food processor, combine the basil, walnuts, garlic, and Parmesan cheese, processing until finely chopped.
3. With the machine running, slowly drizzle in the olive oil until well combined. Season with salt and black pepper to taste.
4. Toss the cooked spaghetti with the walnut pesto.
5. Garnish with cherry tomatoes and extra walnuts if desired, before serving.

## Nutritional Information:

350 Calories - 35g Carbs - 20g Fat - 4g Saturated Fats - 12g Protein - 6g Fibers - 150mg Sodium - 2g Sugar

## Tip:

- You can store leftover pesto in an airtight container in the fridge for up to a week.

## Nutritional Benefits:

- Walnuts are a great source of omega-3 fatty acids which are beneficial for heart health.

# 52. Chickpea Curry

**Prep Time:** 10 minutes | **Cooking Time:** 25 minutes | **Serving Size:** 4

## Ingredients

- 2 tablespoons coconut oil
- 1 onion, diced
- 2 cloves garlic, minced
- 1-inch ginger, minced
- 1 tablespoon curry powder
- 1 teaspoon ground cumin
- 1 teaspoon ground coriander
- 1 can (15-ounce) chickpeas, drained and rinsed
- 1 can (15-ounce) diced tomatoes
- 1 can (13.5-ounce) coconut milk
- Salt and black pepper to taste
- Fresh cilantro and lime wedges for garnish

## Instructions

1. Heat the coconut oil in a large skillet over medium heat. Add the onion, garlic, and ginger, and sauté for 3-5 minutes until the onion is translucent.
2. Stir in the curry powder, cumin, and coriander, and cook for another minute until fragrant.
3. Add the chickpeas, diced tomatoes (with juices), and coconut milk to the skillet, stirring to combine.
4. Bring the mixture to a boil, then reduce the heat and simmer for 15-20 minutes until the curry has thickened.
5. Season with salt and black pepper to taste.
6. Garnish with fresh cilantro and lime wedges before serving.

## Nutritional Information:

350 Calories - 29g Carbs - 24g Fat - 18g Saturated Fats - 9g Protein - 8g Fibers - 480mg Sodium - 6g Sugar

## Tip:

- Add vegetables like spinach or sweet potato for extra nutrition.

## Nutritional Benefits:

- Coconut milk provides healthy fats, but it's high in saturated fats, so it should be consumed in moderation.

# 53. Seafood Paella

**Prep Time:** 15 minutes | **Cooking Time:** 35 minutes | **Serving Size:** 6

## Ingredients

- 2 tablespoons olive oil
- 1 onion, diced
- 3 cloves garlic, minced
- 1 red bell pepper, diced
- 1.5 cups Arborio rice
- 1/4 teaspoon saffron threads
- 1/4 teaspoon paprika
- 1/4 teaspoon black pepper
- 3 cups low-sodium vegetable broth
- 1 cup diced tomatoes
- 1/2 pound shrimp, peeled and deveined
- 1/2 pound mussels, cleaned
- 1/2 pound clams, cleaned
- Fresh parsley and lemon wedges for garnish

## Instructions

1. In a large paella pan or wide skillet, heat the olive oil over medium heat. Add the onion, garlic, and bell pepper, and sauté for 5-7 minutes until the vegetables are softened.
2. Stir in the rice, saffron, paprika, and black pepper, and cook for another 2-3 minutes until the rice is lightly toasted.
3. Pour in the vegetable broth and diced tomatoes, bringing the mixture to a boil. Reduce the heat to low, cover, and simmer for 15-20 minutes until the rice is cooked.
4. Arrange the shrimp, mussels, and clams over the rice, cover, and cook for an additional 10-12 minutes until the seafood is cooked through and the shellfish have opened.
5. Discard any unopened shellfish.
6. Garnish with fresh parsley and lemon wedges before serving.

## Nutritional Information:

310 Calories - 44g Carbs - 6g Fat - 1g Saturated Fats - 20g Protein - 2g Fibers - 300mg Sodium - 4g Sugar

## Tip:

- You can add peas and artichokes for a traditional touch and extra nutrition.

## Nutritional Benefits:

- Seafood is a great source of protein and omega-3 fatty acids which are beneficial for heart health.

# 54. Beat-Steady Beef and Vegetable Stir-fry

**Prep Time:** 15 minutes | **Cooking Time:** 10 minutes | **Serving Size:** 4

## Ingredients

- 1 pound lean beef strips
- 2 tablespoons low-sodium soy sauce
- 1 tablespoon olive oil
- 2 cloves garlic, minced
- 1-inch ginger, minced
- 1 bell pepper, sliced
- 1 carrot, julienned
- 1 zucchini, sliced
- 1/2 cup snap peas
- 2 green onions, sliced
- 1 tablespoon sesame seeds

## Instructions

1. Marinate the beef strips in soy sauce for at least 30 minutes or overnight in the refrigerator.
2. Heat the olive oil in a large skillet or wok over medium-high heat. Add the garlic and ginger, and sauté for about 1 minute until fragrant.
3. Add the marinated beef to the skillet and stir-fry for 3-4 minutes until browned and nearly cooked through.
4. Add the bell pepper, carrot, zucchini, and snap peas to the skillet, and continue to stir-fry for another 4-5 minutes until the vegetables are tender-crisp.
5. Garnish with sliced green onions and sesame seeds before serving.

## Nutritional Information:

300 Calories - 10g Carbs - 12g Fat - 3g Saturated Fats - 35g Protein - 3g Fibers - 450mg Sodium - 5g Sugar

## Tip:

- You can substitute the beef with chicken or tofu for a leaner or vegetarian option.

## Nutritional Benefits:

- Lean beef provides a good amount of protein and essential nutrients like iron and B vitamins without too much saturated fat.

# 55. Rosemary Roasted Chicken

**Prep Time:** 10 minutes | **Cooking Time:** 45 minutes | **Serving Size:** 4

**Ingredients**

- 4 bone-in, skin-on chicken thighs
- 2 tablespoons olive oil
- 2 teaspoons fresh rosemary, minced
- 2 cloves garlic, minced
- Salt and black pepper to taste
- 4-6 baby potatoes, halved
- 2 carrots, sliced
- 1 onion, quartered

**Instructions**

1. Preheat the oven to 425°F (220°C).
2. Rub the chicken thighs with olive oil, rosemary, garlic, salt, and black pepper.
3. Arrange the chicken thighs, potatoes, carrots, and onion in a baking dish.
4. Roast in the preheated oven for 35-45 minutes, or until the chicken is cooked through and the vegetables are tender.
5. Serve warm.

**Nutritional Information:**

410 Calories - 20g Carbs - 24g Fat - 6g Saturated Fats - 30g Protein - 3g Fibers - 200mg Sodium - 5g Sugar

**Tip:**

- Use a meat thermometer to ensure the chicken reaches a safe internal temperature of 165°F (74°C).

**Nutritional Benefits:**

- Rosemary is known for its anti-inflammatory properties and can be a heart-healthy herb to include in your diet.

# 56. Grilled Tuna Steaks

**Prep Time:** 10 minutes | **Cooking Time:** 10 minutes | **Serving Size:** 4

**Ingredients**

- 4 tuna steaks
- 2 tablespoons olive oil
- 1 tablespoon lemon juice
- 2 cloves garlic, minced
- Salt and black pepper to taste
- Fresh parsley for garnish

**Instructions**

1. Preheat the grill to medium-high heat.

2.  In a small bowl, whisk together the olive oil, lemon juice, garlic, salt, and black pepper.

3.  Brush the tuna steaks with the olive oil mixture.

4.  Place the tuna steaks on the grill and cook for about 4-5 minutes on each side for medium, or to your desired level of doneness.

5.  Garnish with fresh parsley before serving.

## Nutritional Information:

210 Calories - 0g Carbs - 7g Fat - 1.5g Saturated Fats - 35g Protein - 0g Fibers - 60mg Sodium - 0g Sugar

## Tip:

*   Avoid overcooking the tuna steaks as they can become dry; it's best when cooked to medium rare to medium.

## Nutritional Benefits:

*   Tuna is a great source of protein and omega-3 fatty acids, which are known to be beneficial for heart health.

# 57. Veggie Loaded Chili

**Prep Time:** 15 minutes | **Cooking Time:** 30 minutes | **Serving Size:** 4

## Ingredients

*   2 tablespoons olive oil
*   1 onion, diced
*   3 cloves garlic, minced
*   2 bell peppers, diced
*   1 zucchini, diced
*   1 carrot, diced
*   2 cans (15 oz each) low-sodium black beans, drained and rinsed
*   1 can (15 oz) low-sodium diced tomatoes
*   1 tablespoon chili powder
*   1 teaspoon cumin
*   1/2 teaspoon smoked paprika
*   Salt and black pepper to taste
*   Fresh cilantro, for garnish

## Instructions

1.  Heat olive oil in a large pot over medium heat. Add onion and garlic, sautéing for about 3 minutes until softened.

2.  Stir in bell peppers, zucchini, and carrot, and continue cooking for another 5 minutes.

3.  Add black beans, diced tomatoes, chili powder, cumin, smoked paprika, salt, and pepper. Stir well to combine.

4.  Bring to a boil, then reduce heat and simmer for 20-25 minutes until the vegetables are tender and the flavors meld.

5.  Garnish with fresh cilantro before serving.

**Nutritional Information:**

230 Calories - 35g Carbs - 7g Fat - 1g Saturated Fats - 10g Protein - 12g Fibers - 230mg Sodium - 6g Sugar

**Tip:**

- This chili can be made in advance and reheated for a quick and easy meal.

**Nutritional Benefits:**

- High in fiber and plant-based protein from the black beans, supporting heart health and digestion.

## 58. Pleaser Lentil Loaf

**Prep Time:** 15 minutes | **Cooking Time:** 45 minutes | **Serving Size:** 6

**Ingredients**

- 2 cups cooked lentils
- 1 onion, finely diced
- 2 cloves garlic, minced
- 1 carrot, grated
- 1/2 cup oats
- 1/2 cup whole wheat bread crumbs
- 2 tablespoons tomato paste
- 1 tablespoon Worcestershire sauce (vegetarian-friendly, if desired)
- 1 teaspoon dried thyme
- Salt and black pepper to taste
- 1/4 cup ketchup, for topping

**Instructions**

1. Preheat the oven to 375°F (190°C).
2. In a large mixing bowl, mash the lentils slightly with a fork or potato masher.
3. Stir in the onion, garlic, carrot, oats, bread crumbs, tomato paste, Worcestershire sauce, dried thyme, salt, and pepper. Mix well until combined.
4. Transfer the mixture to a lined or greased loaf pan, pressing down firmly.
5. Spread the ketchup on top of the lentil mixture.
6. Bake in the preheated oven for 40-45 minutes until the loaf is firm and the edges are slightly crispy.
7. Allow to cool for a few minutes before slicing and serving.

**Nutritional Information:**

220 Calories - 40g Carbs - 2g Fat - 0g Saturated Fats - 12g Protein - 14g Fibers - 250mg Sodium - 6g Sugar

**Tip:**

- Leftovers can be refrigerated and reheated for a quick meal later in the week.

**Nutritional Benefits:**

- Lentils are a great source of plant-based protein and are rich in heart-healthy fiber.

# 59. Nourish Bowl

**Prep Time:** 15 minutes | **Cooking Time:** 0 minutes | **Serving Size:** 2

## Ingredients

- 2 cups cooked quinoa
- 1 cup chickpeas, cooked and drained
- 1/2 cup cherry tomatoes, halved
- 1/2 cup cucumber, diced
- 1/4 cup red onion, finely diced
- 1/4 cup kalamata olives, pitted and halved
- 1/4 cup feta cheese, crumbled
- 2 tablespoons extra virgin olive oil
- 1 tablespoon lemon juice
- Salt and black pepper to taste
- Fresh parsley, for garnish

## Instructions

1. Divide the cooked quinoa between two bowls.
2. Top each bowl with equal amounts of chickpeas, cherry tomatoes, cucumber, red onion, olives, and feta cheese.
3. In a small bowl, whisk together the olive oil, lemon juice, salt, and pepper. Drizzle over each nourish bowl.
4. Garnish with fresh parsley before serving.

## Nutritional Information:

360 Calories - 40g Carbs - 16g Fat - 4g Saturated Fats - 12g Protein - 8g Fibers - 350mg Sodium - 6g Sugar

## Tip:

- This nourish bowl is perfect for meal prep - prepare the ingredients in advance and assemble when ready to eat.

## Nutritional Benefits:

- Chickpeas provide plant-based protein and fiber, supporting heart health and digestion.

# 60. Garlic Parmesan Zoodles

**Prep Time:** 10 minutes | **Cooking Time:** 10 minutes | **Serving Size:** 2

**Ingredients**

- 4 medium zucchinis
- 1 tablespoon olive oil
- 3 cloves garlic, minced
- 1/4 cup grated Parmesan cheese
- 1 tablespoon fresh lemon juice
- Salt and black pepper to taste
- Fresh parsley, finely chopped for garnish
- Cherry tomatoes, halved for garnish

**Instructions**

1. Spiralize the zucchinis to create zoodles, or use a vegetable peeler to create thin ribbons. Set aside.
2. In a large skillet, heat the olive oil over medium heat. Add the minced garlic and sauté for about 1 minute until fragrant.
3. Add the zoodles to the skillet and toss to coat in the garlic oil. Cook for about 5-7 minutes until the zoodles are tender but still have a bit of crunch.
4. Remove from heat and stir in the Parmesan cheese, lemon juice, salt, and black pepper.
5. Divide between two plates, garnish with fresh parsley and cherry tomatoes, and serve immediately.

**Nutritional Information:**

180 Calories - 12g Carbs - 12g Fat - 3g Saturated Fats - 9g Protein - 4g Fibers - 250mg Sodium - 8g Sugar

**Tip:**

- Avoid overcooking the zoodles to prevent them from becoming mushy.

**Nutritional Benefits:**

- Olive oil and Parmesan provide healthy fats which can help to lower bad cholesterol levels.

# Chapter 7: Snacks and Sides Recipes

## 61. Heart-Happy Hummus

**Prep Time:** 10 minutes | **Cooking Time:** 0 minutes | **Serving Size:** 4

**Ingredients**

- 1 can (15 oz) chickpeas, rinsed and drained
- 2 cloves garlic, minced
- 2 tablespoons tahini
- 2 tablespoons lemon juice
- 2 tablespoons extra virgin olive oil
- Salt and pepper to taste
- Paprika, for garnish
- Fresh parsley, for garnish

**Instructions**

1. In a food processor, combine the chickpeas, garlic, tahini, lemon juice, and olive oil. Process until smooth and creamy, adding a little water if necessary to reach the desired consistency.
2. Season with salt and pepper to taste.
3. Transfer to a serving bowl, and garnish with a sprinkle of paprika and fresh parsley.
4. Serve with fresh vegetable sticks or whole grain crackers.

**Nutritional Information:**

165 Calories - 13g Carbs - 10g Fat - 1.5g Saturated Fats - 5g Protein - 4g Fibers - 10mg Sodium - 1g Sugar

**Tip:**

- Store leftovers in an airtight container in the fridge for up to a week.

**Nutritional Benefits:**

- Chickpeas are a great source of plant-based protein and dietary fiber which can aid in heart health.

## 62. Cardio-Careful Carrot Sticks

**Prep Time:** 10 minutes | **Cooking Time:** 0 minutes | **Serving Size:** 4

**Ingredients**

- 4 large carrots
- 1 tablespoon olive oil
- 1/4 teaspoon salt
- 1/4 teaspoon black pepper
- 1/4 teaspoon paprika

**Instructions**

1. Wash, peel, and cut the carrots into stick shapes.
2. Toss the carrot sticks with olive oil, salt, black pepper, and paprika.
3. Serve immediately or store in an airtight container in the fridge for up to a week.

**Nutritional Information:**

45 Calories - 6g Carbs - 2.5g Fat - 0g Saturated Fats - 0g Protein - 2g Fibers - 150mg Sodium - 3g Sugar

**Tip:**

- These carrot sticks are great for dipping in hummus or guacamole.

**Nutritional Benefits:**

- Carrots are a rich source of beta-carotene, a powerful antioxidant that can help reduce the risk of heart disease.

## 63. Loving Protein Bars

**Prep Time:** 15 minutes | **Cooking Time:** 0 minutes | **Serving Size:** 8 bars

**Ingredients**

- 1 cup dates, pitted
- 1/4 cup honey
- 1/4 cup almond butter
- 1 cup rolled oats
- 1 cup almonds, chopped
- 1/2 cup protein powder

**Instructions**

1. Line an 8x8-inch baking dish with parchment paper.
2. In a food processor, process the dates until they form a ball.
3. In a large mixing bowl, mix the honey and almond butter. Microwave for about 30 seconds to soften, then stir in the dates.
4. Add the oats, almonds, and protein powder to the mixture, and stir well to combine.
5. Transfer the mixture to the prepared baking dish, and press down firmly to create an even layer.
6. Chill in the refrigerator for at least 1 hour, then cut into 8 bars.

**Nutritional Information:**

235 Calories - 30g Carbs - 10g Fat - 1g Saturated Fats - 10g Protein - 5g Fibers - 15mg Sodium - 20g Sugar

**Tip:**

- These bars can be stored in an airtight container in the fridge for up to 2 weeks.

**Nutritional Benefits:**

- Almonds are a heart-healthy nut, providing a good amount of monounsaturated fats.

# 64. Heart's Delight Dried Fruit Mix

**Prep Time:** 10 minutes | **Cooking Time:** 0 minutes | **Serving Size:** 10

**Ingredients**

- 1 cup dried apricots, chopped
- 1 cup dried figs, chopped
- 1/2 cup dried cranberries
- 1/2 cup raisins
- 1/2 cup almonds
- 1/2 cup walnuts

**Instructions**

1. In a large mixing bowl, combine all the ingredients and toss well to mix.
2. Store in an airtight container at room temperature for up to 2 weeks.
3. Serve as a quick snack or as a topping on yogurt, oatmeal, or salads.

**Nutritional Information:**

170 Calories - 30g Carbs - 7g Fat - 0.5g Saturated Fats - 3g Protein - 4g Fibers - 5mg Sodium - 20g Sugar

**Tip:**

- Ensure the dried fruits are free from added sugars to keep this mix heart-healthy.

**Nutritional Benefits:**

- Dried fruits provide essential vitamins and minerals including potassium which is beneficial for heart health.

# 65. Tender Love Trail Mix

**Prep Time:** 10 minutes | **Cooking Time:** 0 minutes | **Serving Size:** 8

**Ingredients**

- 1/2 cup almonds
- 1/2 cup walnuts
- 1/4 cup pumpkin seeds
- 1/4 cup sunflower seeds
- 1/2 cup dried cherries
- 1/4 cup dark chocolate chips

**Instructions**

1. In a large mixing bowl, combine all the ingredients and toss well to mix.
2. Store in an airtight container at room temperature for up to 2 weeks.
3. Serve as a snack or use as a topping on yogurt or oatmeal.

**Nutritional Information:**

200 Calories - 12g Carbs - 16g Fat - 3g Saturated Fats - 6g Protein - 3g Fibers - 5mg Sodium - 6g Sugar

**Tip:**

- Opt for dark chocolate with at least 70% cocoa to reap the heart-healthy benefits.

**Nutritional Benefits:**

- Dark chocolate is known to be rich in antioxidants and may help improve heart health when consumed in moderation.

# 66. Hemp Seed Crackers

**Prep Time:** 15 minutes | **Cooking Time:** 15 minutes | **Serving Size:** 8 (about 4 crackers each)

**Ingredients**

- 1/2 cup hemp seeds
- 1/2 cup sunflower seeds
- 1/4 cup sesame seeds
- 1/4 cup chia seeds
- 1 cup water
- 1/2 teaspoon salt
- 1/4 teaspoon black pepper
- 1/4 teaspoon garlic powder

**Instructions**

1. Preheat the oven to 350°F (175°C) and line a baking sheet with parchment paper.
2. In a mixing bowl, combine all the seeds.
3. Stir in the water, salt, black pepper, and garlic powder, and let sit for 15-20 minutes, or until the chia seeds have gelled and the mixture holds together.

4. Spread the mixture thinly on the prepared baking sheet, and bake for 15-20 minutes, or until golden and crisp.

5. Allow to cool completely before breaking into crackers.

**Nutritional Information:**

135 Calories - 4g Carbs - 11g Fat - 1g Saturated Fats - 6g Protein - 4g Fibers - 150mg Sodium - 0g Sugar

**Tip:**

- Store the crackers in an airtight container for up to a week.

**Nutritional Benefits:**

- Chia seeds provide dietary fiber which can help lower cholesterol levels and improve heart health.

# 67. Wholesome Heart Walnut Mix

**Prep Time:** 5 minutes | **Cooking Time:** 10 minutes | **Serving Size:** 8

**Ingredients**

- 2 cups walnuts
- 1 tablespoon olive oil
- 1/2 teaspoon sea salt
- 1/4 teaspoon black pepper
- 1/4 teaspoon paprika
- 1/4 teaspoon garlic powder

**Instructions**

1. Preheat the oven to 350°F (175°C). Line a baking sheet with parchment paper.

2. In a medium-sized bowl, toss the walnuts with olive oil, sea salt, black pepper, paprika, and garlic powder until well coated.

3. Spread the walnuts on the prepared baking sheet in a single layer.

4. Bake for 10-12 minutes, or until the walnuts are toasted and fragrant.

5. Allow to cool completely before serving or storing in an airtight container.

**Nutritional Information:**

200 Calories - 4g Carbs - 20g Fat - 2g Saturated Fats - 4g Protein - 2g Fibers - 150mg Sodium - 1g Sugar

**Tip:**

- Walnuts can be replaced with any other nuts like almonds, pecans, or mixed nuts for variety.

**Nutritional Benefits:**

- Olive oil is known for its heart-healthy monounsaturated fats which may help reduce inflammation and lower cholesterol levels.

## 68. Beat-Steady Baked Kale Chips

**Prep Time:** 10 minutes | **Cooking Time:** 15 minutes | **Serving Size:** 4

**Ingredients**

- 1 bunch of kale, stems removed and torn into bite-sized pieces
- 1 tablespoon olive oil
- 1/4 teaspoon sea salt
- 1/4 teaspoon black pepper

**Instructions**

1. Preheat the oven to 350°F (175°C). Line a baking sheet with parchment paper.
2. In a large bowl, toss the kale pieces with olive oil, sea salt, and black pepper until well coated.
3. Spread the kale in a single layer on the prepared baking sheet.
4. Bake for 10-15 minutes, or until the edges are slightly brown but not burnt.
5. Allow to cool before serving. Store any leftovers in an airtight container.

**Nutritional Information:**

50 Calories - 4g Carbs - 4g Fat - 0.5g Saturated Fats - 1g Protein - 1g Fibers - 150mg Sodium - 0g Sugar

**Tip:**

- Ensure kale is thoroughly dried after washing to achieve crispy chips.

**Nutritional Benefits:**

- Kale is a nutrient-dense vegetable rich in vitamins A, C, K, and various antioxidants that support heart health.

## 69. Herb Roasted Nuts

**Prep Time:** 5 minutes | **Cooking Time:** 15 minutes | **Serving Size:** 8

**Ingredients**

- 2 cups mixed nuts (almonds, walnuts, pecans)
- 1 tablespoon olive oil
- 1/2 teaspoon sea salt
- 1/4 teaspoon black pepper
- 1/2 teaspoon dried rosemary
- 1/2 teaspoon dried thyme

**Instructions**

1. Preheat the oven to 350°F (175°C). Line a baking sheet with parchment paper.
2. In a medium bowl, toss the mixed nuts with olive oil, sea salt, black pepper, dried rosemary, and dried thyme until well coated.
3. Spread the nut mixture on the prepared baking sheet in a single layer.
4. Bake for 10-15 minutes, or until the nuts are toasted and fragrant.
5. Allow to cool completely before serving or storing in an airtight container.

**Nutritional Information:**

200 Calories - 6g Carbs - 20g Fat - 2g Saturated Fats - 5g Protein - 3g Fibers - 150mg Sodium - 1g Sugar

**Tip:**

- Any combination of your favorite nuts can be used in this recipe.

**Nutritional Benefits:**

- Herbs like rosemary and thyme provide flavor without added sodium, promoting better heart health.

# 70. Lemon Zest Popcorn

**Prep Time:** 5 minutes | **Cooking Time:** 5 minutes | **Serving Size:** 4

**Ingredients**

- 1/2 cup popcorn kernels
- 1 tablespoon coconut oil
- Zest of 1 lemon
- 1/2 teaspoon sea salt
- 1/4 teaspoon black pepper

**Instructions**

1. In a large pot, heat coconut oil over medium heat.
2. Once the oil is hot, add the popcorn kernels and cover the pot.
3. Shake the pot occasionally to prevent the kernels from burning. Once the popping slows down, remove the pot from heat and let it sit covered until the popping stops completely.
4. Transfer the popcorn to a large bowl, and while it's still hot, toss it with lemon zest, sea salt, and black pepper.
5. Serve immediately or store in an airtight container once cooled.

**Nutritional Information:**

110 Calories - 12g Carbs - 6g Fat - 5g Saturated Fats - 2g Protein - 2g Fibers - 290mg Sodium - 0g Sugar

**Tip:**

- Use a popcorn maker if available for an even easier preparation.

**Nutritional Benefits:**

- Lemon zest not only adds flavor but also a small amount of vitamin C which is an antioxidant that can promote heart health.

# 71. Tomato Basil Bruschetta

**Prep Time:** 15 minutes | **Cooking Time:** 10 minutes | **Serving Size:** 4

**Ingredients**

- 1 baguette, sliced into 1/2-inch thick rounds
- 2 cups cherry tomatoes, quartered
- 1/4 cup fresh basil leaves, chopped
- 2 tablespoons olive oil, divided
- 1 garlic clove, minced
- Salt and pepper to taste

**Instructions**

1. Preheat the oven to 400°F (200°C).
2. Place the baguette slices on a baking sheet and brush one side of each slice with 1 tablespoon of olive oil.
3. Bake for about 5-10 minutes, or until the bread is golden and crispy.
4. In a medium bowl, combine the cherry tomatoes, basil, the remaining olive oil, garlic, salt, and pepper.
5. Spoon the tomato mixture onto the toasted baguette slices, and serve immediately.

**Nutritional Information:**

200 Calories - 26g Carbs - 9g Fat - 1.5g Saturated Fats - 5g Protein - 2g Fibers - 340mg Sodium - 3g Sugar

**Tip:**

- Fresh basil is key for a burst of flavor in this recipe.

**Nutritional Benefits:**

- Tomatoes are a good source of vitamins A and C and potassium, and are known for their antioxidant lycopene, which can help prevent heart disease.

# 72. Whole Grain Toasties

**Prep Time:** 5 minutes | **Cooking Time:** 10 minutes | **Serving Size:** 4

**Ingredients**

- 8 slices of whole grain bread
- 2 tablespoons olive oil
- 1/2 teaspoon garlic powder
- 1/4 teaspoon sea salt
- 1/4 teaspoon black pepper

**Instructions**

1. Preheat the oven to 350°F (175°C).
2. Brush both sides of each bread slice with olive oil.
3. Sprinkle garlic powder, sea salt, and black pepper over the bread slices.
4. Place the bread slices on a baking sheet and bake for 5-10 minutes, or until they are crispy and golden.
5. Serve immediately or allow to cool and store in an airtight container for later use.

**Nutritional Information:**

200 Calories - 26g Carbs - 9g Fat - 1.5g Saturated Fats - 6g Protein - 4g Fibers - 300mg Sodium - 4g Sugar

**Tip:**

- These toasties can be enjoyed with hummus, guacamole, or any dip of your choice.

**Nutritional Benefits:**

- Whole grain bread is rich in fiber which can help lower cholesterol and improve heart health.

# 73. Heartful Honey Almond Clusters

**Prep Time:** 10 minutes | **Cooking Time:** 15 minutes | **Serving Size:** 8

**Ingredients**

- 2 cups almonds, roughly chopped
- 2 tablespoons honey
- 1 teaspoon vanilla extract
- A pinch of sea salt

**Instructions**

1. Preheat the oven to 350°F (175°C) and line a baking sheet with parchment paper.
2. In a medium bowl, mix the almonds, honey, vanilla extract, and sea salt until the almonds are well-coated.
3. Spread the almond mixture onto the prepared baking sheet in a single layer.
4. Bake for about 12-15 minutes, or until the almonds are toasted and the honey has caramelized.
5. Allow to cool completely on the baking sheet, then break apart into clusters.

**Nutritional Information:**

210 Calories - 8g Carbs - 18g Fat - 1.5g Saturated Fats - 8g Protein - 4g Fibers - 30mg Sodium - 5g Sugar

**Tip:**

- Store in an airtight container for up to 2 weeks.

**Nutritional Benefits:**

- Honey offers natural sweetness while providing some antioxidant properties.

# 74. Tender Touch Turmeric Roasted Chickpeas

**Prep Time:** 10 minutes | **Cooking Time:** 25 minutes | **Serving Size:** 4

## Ingredients

- 2 cans (15 oz each) chickpeas, drained, rinsed and patted dry
- 2 tablespoons olive oil
- 1 teaspoon turmeric
- 1/2 teaspoon paprika
- Salt and pepper to taste

## Instructions

1. Preheat the oven to 400°F (200°C) and line a baking sheet with parchment paper.
2. In a medium bowl, toss the chickpeas with olive oil, turmeric, paprika, salt, and pepper.
3. Spread the chickpeas out on the prepared baking sheet in a single layer.
4. Roast for about 20-25 minutes, stirring halfway through, until crispy and golden.
5. Allow to cool before serving.

## Nutritional Information:

210 Calories - 26g Carbs - 9g Fat - 1g Saturated Fats - 8g Protein - 7g Fibers - 300mg Sodium - 5g Sugar

## Tip:

- These roasted chickpeas can be enjoyed on their own or tossed into salads for added crunch.

## Nutritional Benefits:

- Chickpeas are a good source of protein and fiber which can help improve heart health.

# 75. Nut Butter Bites

**Prep Time:** 15 minutes | **Cooking Time:** 0 minutes | **Serving Size:** 12 bites

## Ingredients

- 1 cup rolled oats
- 1/2 cup almond butter or peanut butter
- 1/4 cup honey
- 1/4 cup dark chocolate chips
- 2 tablespoons chia seeds
- 2 tablespoons flaxseeds, ground
- A pinch of sea salt

## Instructions

1. In a large bowl, mix together the rolled oats, nut butter, honey, chocolate chips, chia seeds, flaxseeds, and sea salt.
2. Refrigerate the mixture for about 30 minutes to firm up slightly, which will make it easier to shape.
3. Using your hands, shape the mixture into 12 equal-sized balls.
4. Store the bites in an airtight container in the refrigerator for up to 1 week.

## Nutritional Information:

150 Calories - 14g Carbs - 9g Fat - 2g Saturated Fats - 4g Protein - 3g Fibers - 25mg Sodium - 7g Sugar

## Tip:

- Substitute the chocolate chips with raisins or dried cranberries for a different taste.

## Nutritional Benefits:

- Nut butter is a source of protein and heart-healthy fats.

# 76. Pumpkin Seed Crunch

**Prep Time:** 10 minutes | **Cooking Time:** 12 minutes | **Serving Size:** 6

**Ingredients**

- 2 cups raw pumpkin seeds
- 1 tablespoon olive oil
- 1/2 teaspoon smoked paprika
- 1/4 teaspoon cayenne pepper
- Sea salt to taste

**Instructions**

1. Preheat the oven to 350°F (175°C) and line a baking sheet with parchment paper.
2. In a medium bowl, mix the pumpkin seeds with olive oil, smoked paprika, cayenne pepper, and sea salt.
3. Spread the seeds in a single layer on the prepared baking sheet.
4. Bake for about 10-12 minutes or until golden and crisp.
5. Allow to cool before serving or storing in an airtight container.

**Nutritional Information:**

200 Calories - 4g Carbs - 18g Fat - 3.5g Saturated Fats - 10g Protein - 2g Fibers - 5mg Sodium - 0g Sugar

**Tip:**

- Store in an airtight container for up to 2 weeks.

**Nutritional Benefits:**

- Pumpkin seeds are rich in antioxidants, magnesium, and fatty acids that are beneficial for heart health.

# 77. Wholesome Guacamole

**Prep Time:** 10 minutes | **Cooking Time:** 0 minutes | **Serving Size:** 4

## Ingredients

- 3 ripe avocados, peeled and pitted
- 1 small red onion, finely chopped
- 1 jalapeño, seeded and minced (optional)
- Juice of 1 lime
- 1/4 cup fresh cilantro, chopped
- Salt and pepper to taste

## Instructions

1. In a medium bowl, mash the avocados with a fork to your desired consistency.
2. Stir in the red onion, jalapeño (if using), lime juice, cilantro, salt, and pepper.
3. Cover with plastic wrap, pressing it directly onto the surface of the guacamole to prevent browning.
4. Refrigerate for at least 30 minutes to allow the flavors to meld, or serve immediately.

## Nutritional Information:

200 Calories - 12g Carbs - 18g Fat - 3g Saturated Fats - 3g Protein - 9g Fibers - 10mg Sodium - 1g Sugar

## Tip:

- Guacamole is best enjoyed fresh but can be refrigerated for up to 1 day.

## Nutritional Benefits:

- Avocados are rich in monounsaturated fats which are heart-healthy fats.

# 78. Hearty Seed Mix

**Prep Time:** 5 minutes | **Cooking Time:** 15 minutes | **Serving Size:** 8

## Ingredients

- 1 cup raw sunflower seeds
- 1 cup raw pumpkin seeds
- 1/2 cup chia seeds
- 1/2 cup flaxseeds
- 2 tablespoons olive oil
- 1/2 teaspoon sea salt
- 1/4 teaspoon black pepper

## Instructions

1. Preheat the oven to 350°F (175°C) and line a baking sheet with parchment paper.
2. In a large bowl, mix together the sunflower seeds, pumpkin seeds, chia seeds, flaxseeds, olive oil, sea salt, and black pepper.
3. Spread the seed mixture out in a single layer on the prepared baking sheet.
4. Bake for about 15 minutes, stirring halfway through, until the seeds are toasted.
5. Allow to cool completely before storing in an airtight container.

## Nutritional Information:

200 Calories - 8g Carbs - 17g Fat - 2g Saturated Fats - 7g Protein - 5g Fibers - 150mg Sodium - 0g Sugar

## Tip:

- This seed mix can be enjoyed on its own, sprinkled over salads, or mixed into yogurt.

## Nutritional Benefits:

- Seeds are a great source of heart-healthy fats, protein, and fiber.

# 79. Pleasing Pea and Mint Dip

**Prep Time:** 10 minutes | **Cooking Time:** 0 minutes | **Serving Size:** 4

## Ingredients

- 2 cups frozen peas, thawed
- 1/4 cup fresh mint leaves
- 2 tablespoons olive oil
- 2 tablespoons lemon juice
- Salt and black pepper to taste
- Optional: 1 clove garlic, minced

## Instructions

1. In a food processor, combine the peas, mint leaves, olive oil, lemon juice, and garlic (if using). Process until smooth.
2. Season with salt and black pepper to taste, and process again to mix.
3. Transfer to a serving bowl and serve immediately, or cover and refrigerate until ready to serve.

## Nutritional Information:

100 Calories - 12g Carbs - 5g Fat - 0.5g Saturated Fats - 4g Protein - 4g Fibers - 5mg Sodium - 4g Sugar

## Tip:

- This dip can be made a day in advance and kept refrigerated.

## Nutritional Benefits:

- Mint is known for its digestive benefits and provides a refreshing flavor.

# 80. Herb-Infused Olives

**Prep Time:** 5 minutes | **Cooking Time:** 0 minutes | **Serving Size:** 4

**Ingredients**

- 1 cup mixed olives (Kalamata, green, black)
- 1/4 cup extra virgin olive oil
- Zest of 1 lemon
- 2 cloves garlic, minced
- 1 teaspoon dried rosemary
- 1 teaspoon dried thyme

**Instructions**

1. In a medium bowl, combine the olives, olive oil, lemon zest, garlic, rosemary, and thyme.
2. Mix well to ensure the olives are well-coated with the herbs and oil.
3. Cover and refrigerate for at least 2 hours, or overnight for better flavor infusion.
4. Serve chilled or at room temperature.

**Nutritional Information:**

150 Calories - 2g Carbs - 16g Fat - 2g Saturated Fats - 0g Protein - 1g Fibers - 300mg Sodium - 0g Sugar

**Tip:**

- These herb-infused olives make a great accompaniment to a cheese platter or as a stand-alone snack.

**Nutritional Benefits:**

- Olives and olive oil are rich in heart-healthy monounsaturated fats and antioxidants.

# Chapter 8:    Dessert Recipes

## 81. Heart-Sweet Berry Compote

**Prep Time:** 5 minutes | **Cooking Time:** 15 minutes | **Serving Size:** 4

**Ingredients**

- 2 cups mixed berries (strawberries, blueberries, raspberries)
- 2 tablespoons pure maple syrup or honey
- 1 teaspoon lemon zest
- 1 tablespoon lemon juice

**Instructions**

1. In a medium saucepan, combine the mixed berries, maple syrup or honey, lemon zest, and lemon juice.
2. Bring to a simmer over medium heat, stirring occasionally.
3. Reduce heat to low and continue to simmer for about 10-15 minutes, or until the berries have softened and the mixture has thickened slightly.
4. Allow to cool before serving over heart-healthy pancakes, oatmeal, or yogurt.

**Nutritional Information:**

70 Calories - 17g Carbs - 0g Fat - 0g Saturated Fats - 0g Protein - 3g Fibers - 0mg Sodium - 13g Sugar

**Tip:**

- Feel free to use frozen berries if fresh berries are not available.

**Nutritional Benefits:**

- Berries are rich in antioxidants and dietary fiber which are beneficial for heart health.

# 82. Lemon Bars

**Prep Time:** 20 minutes | **Cooking Time:** 25 minutes | **Serving Size:** 9

**Ingredients**

- 1 cup whole wheat flour
- 1/4 cup coconut oil, melted
- 1/4 cup pure maple syrup
- 1/4 teaspoon salt
- 4 large eggs
- 1/2 cup fresh lemon juice
- 1/4 cup honey
- 2 teaspoons lemon zest

**Instructions**

1. Preheat the oven to 350°F (175°C) and line a 8x8-inch baking dish with parchment paper.
2. In a medium bowl, combine the whole wheat flour, coconut oil, maple syrup, and salt to form a dough.
3. Press the dough evenly into the bottom of the prepared baking dish and bake for about 10-12 minutes, or until lightly golden.
4. In another bowl, whisk together the eggs, lemon juice, honey, and lemon zest until well combined.
5. Pour the lemon mixture over the baked crust and return to the oven for an additional 12-15 minutes, or until the filling is set.
6. Allow to cool completely before cutting into bars and serving.

**Nutritional Information:**

190 Calories - 25g Carbs - 9g Fat - 6g Saturated Fats - 5g Protein - 2g Fibers - 85mg Sodium - 14g Sugar

**Tip:**

- Store any leftovers in an airtight container in the refrigerator for up to 3 days.

**Nutritional Benefits:**

- Using whole wheat flour and natural sweeteners provides a healthier alternative to traditional lemon bar recipes.

# 83. Tender Heart Chocolate Avocado Mousse

**Prep Time:** 10 minutes | **Cooking Time:** 0 minutes | **Serving Size:** 4

## Ingredients

- 2 ripe avocados, pitted and peeled
- 1/4 cup unsweetened cocoa powder
- 1/4 cup pure maple syrup or honey
- 1/2 teaspoon vanilla extract
- Optional: Fresh berries and mint leaves for garnish

## Instructions

1. In a food processor, combine the avocados, cocoa powder, maple syrup or honey, and vanilla extract.
2. Process until smooth and creamy, scraping down the sides of the bowl as necessary.
3. Transfer the mousse to serving dishes and refrigerate for at least 1 hour, or until chilled.
4. Garnish with fresh berries and mint leaves before serving, if desired.

## Nutritional Information:

210 Calories - 27g Carbs - 13g Fat - 2g Saturated Fats - 3g Protein - 9g Fibers - 10mg Sodium - 15g Sugar

## Tip:

- This mousse can be made a day in advance and kept refrigerated until ready to serve.

## Nutritional Benefits:

- Avocado adds a creamy texture while providing heart-healthy monounsaturated fats.

# 84. Honey Almond Biscotti

**Prep Time:** 20 minutes | **Cooking Time:** 40 minutes | **Serving Size:** 15

**Ingredients**

- 1 cup whole wheat flour
- 1/2 cup almond flour
- 1/2 teaspoon baking powder
- 1/4 teaspoon salt
- 1/4 cup honey
- 2 large eggs
- 1 teaspoon vanilla extract
- 1/2 cup almonds, chopped

**Instructions**

1. Preheat the oven to 350°F (175°C) and line a baking sheet with parchment paper.
2. In a medium bowl, combine whole wheat flour, almond flour, baking powder, and salt.
3. In a separate bowl, whisk together honey, eggs, and vanilla extract until well combined.
4. Gradually add the dry ingredients to the wet ingredients, stirring until a dough forms.
5. Fold in the chopped almonds.
6. Transfer the dough to the prepared baking sheet and shape into a log about 12 inches long and 3 inches wide.
7. Bake for 25-30 minutes or until lightly golden and firm to the touch.
8. Allow to cool for 10 minutes, then slice the log into 1/2-inch thick slices.
9. Place slices cut side down on the baking sheet and bake for an additional 10-12 minutes, or until crispy.

**Nutritional Information:**

90 Calories - 12g Carbs - 4g Fat - 0.5g Saturated Fats - 3g Protein - 2g Fibers - 55mg Sodium - 6g Sugar

**Tip:**

- Biscotti can be stored in an airtight container for up to 2 weeks.

**Nutritional Benefits:**

- Almond flour and almonds provide heart-healthy fats and protein.

## 85. Heartful Herbal Tea Infused Sorbet

**Prep Time:** 10 minutes | **Cooking Time:** 0 minutes (4 hours freezing time) | **Serving Size:** 4

### Ingredients

- 2 cups brewed herbal tea (such as chamomile or peppermint)
- 1/4 cup honey or maple syrup
- 1 tablespoon lemon juice

### Instructions

1. In a mixing bowl, combine the brewed herbal tea, honey or maple syrup, and lemon juice.
2. Pour the mixture into a shallow dish and place in the freezer.
3. Every 30 minutes, stir the mixture with a fork to break up any ice crystals, until the sorbet is frozen and fluffy (about 4 hours).
4. Scoop and serve immediately.

### Nutritional Information:

60 Calories - 16g Carbs - 0g Fat - 0g Saturated Fats - 0g Protein - 0g Fibers - 5mg Sodium - 15g Sugar

### Tip:

- Experiment with different types of herbal teas to find your favorite flavor combination.

### Nutritional Benefits:

- Herbal teas offer a variety of health benefits including anti-inflammatory properties and digestive aid.

## 86. Tender Touch Turmeric Pumpkin Pie

**Prep Time:** 20 minutes | **Cooking Time:** 60 minutes | **Serving Size:** 8

### Ingredients

- 1 whole wheat pie crust
- 1 can (15 oz) pumpkin puree
- 1/4 cup honey or maple syrup
- 2 large eggs
- 1/2 cup unsweetened almond milk
- 1 teaspoon ground cinnamon
- 1/2 teaspoon ground ginger
- 1/4 teaspoon ground turmeric
- 1/4 teaspoon ground nutmeg
- Optional: Whipped coconut cream for serving

### Instructions

1. Preheat the oven to 350°F (175°C) and place the pie crust in a 9-inch pie dish.
2. In a large mixing bowl, combine pumpkin puree, honey or maple syrup, eggs, almond milk, cinnamon, ginger, turmeric, and nutmeg.
3. Whisk until smooth and well combined.

4.  Pour the pumpkin mixture into the prepared pie crust and smooth the top with a spatula.

5.  Bake for 55-60 minutes, or until the filling is set and the crust is lightly golden.

6.  Allow to cool completely before slicing and serving with a dollop of whipped coconut cream, if desired.

**Nutritional Information:**

150 Calories - 25g Carbs - 5g Fat - 2g Saturated Fats - 4g Protein - 3g Fibers - 135mg Sodium - 12g Sugar

**Tip:**

- This pie can be made a day in advance and kept refrigerated until ready to serve.

**Nutritional Benefits:**

- Turmeric and ginger are known for their anti-inflammatory properties and are beneficial for heart health.

# 87. Hazelnut Truffles

**Prep Time:** 20 minutes | **Cooking Time:** 0 minutes (2 hours chilling time) | **Serving Size:** 12

**Ingredients**

- 1 cup hazelnuts, roasted and skinned

- 1/4 cup unsweetened cocoa powder

- 2 tablespoons honey or maple syrup

- 1/2 teaspoon vanilla extract

- A pinch of sea salt

- Optional: extra cocoa powder or crushed hazelnuts for coating

**Instructions**

1.  In a food processor, blend the hazelnuts until they become a fine meal.

2.  Add cocoa powder, honey, vanilla extract, and salt. Process until the mixture comes together and forms a dough.

3.  Chill the dough in the refrigerator for about 30 minutes to firm up.

4.  Roll the dough into small balls, about 1-inch in diameter.

5.  If desired, roll the truffles in extra cocoa powder or crushed hazelnuts for an extra touch.

6.  Store in an airtight container in the refrigerator for up to a week.

**Nutritional Information:**

90 Calories - 7g Carbs - 7g Fat - 0.5g Saturated Fats - 2g Protein - 2g Fibers - 20mg Sodium - 4g Sugar

**Tip:**

- Experiment by adding a small amount of orange zest or replacing vanilla with almond extract for a different flavor profile.

**Nutritional Benefits:**

- Hazelnuts are a great source of heart-healthy fats and antioxidants which are beneficial for heart health.

# 88. Lavender Panna Cotta

**Prep Time:** 15 minutes | **Cooking Time:** 5 minutes (4 hours chilling time) | **Serving Size:** 4

## Ingredients

- 1 can (13.5 oz) full-fat coconut milk
- 2 teaspoons dried culinary lavender
- 3 tablespoons honey or maple syrup
- 1 tablespoon gelatin (or agar-agar for a vegan option)
- 1 teaspoon vanilla extract
- Fresh berries for garnish

## Instructions

1. In a medium saucepan, heat coconut milk and lavender over medium heat until it starts to simmer. Remove from heat and let it steep for about 15 minutes.
2. Strain out the lavender and return the coconut milk to the saucepan.
3. Whisk in the honey or maple syrup.
4. Sprinkle gelatin over the coconut milk mixture and let it sit for 5 minutes to soften.
5. Heat the mixture over low heat, whisking constantly, until the gelatin has fully dissolved.
6. Remove from heat and stir in the vanilla extract.
7. Pour the mixture into ramekins or silicone molds and refrigerate for at least 4 hours, or until set.
8. Serve chilled, garnished with fresh berries.

## Nutritional Information:

200 Calories - 17g Carbs - 14g Fat - 12g Saturated Fats - 2g Protein - 0g Fibers - 15mg Sodium - 14g Sugar

## Tip:

- For a vegan version, use agar-agar in place of gelatin, following the package instructions for substitution amounts.

## Nutritional Benefits:

- Coconut milk provides healthy fats that can help lower bad cholesterol levels.

# 89. Nutty Apple Crisp

**Prep Time:** 15 minutes | **Cooking Time:** 45 minutes | **Serving Size:** 6

## Ingredients

- 4 large apples, peeled, cored, and sliced
- 1 tablespoon lemon juice
- 1/2 cup old-fashioned oats
- 1/4 cup almond flour
- 1/4 cup walnuts, chopped
- 1/4 cup coconut sugar or brown sugar
- 1/4 teaspoon cinnamon
- 1/4 teaspoon nutmeg
- 2 tablespoons coconut oil, melted

## Instructions

1. Preheat the oven to 350°F (175°C) and grease a baking dish.
2. Toss the sliced apples with lemon juice and spread them out in the prepared baking dish.
3. In a mixing bowl, combine oats, almond flour, walnuts, sugar, cinnamon, and nutmeg.
4. Stir in the melted coconut oil until the mixture resembles coarse crumbs.
5. Sprinkle the oat mixture evenly over the apples.
6. Bake for 40-45 minutes, or until the topping is golden and the apples are tender.
7. Serve warm, optionally topped with a scoop of heart-healthy vanilla ice cream or a dollop of coconut whipped cream.

**Nutritional Information:**

200 Calories - 29g Carbs - 10g Fat - 6g Saturated Fats - 3g Protein - 4g Fibers - 0mg Sodium - 20g Sugar

**Tip:**

- Experiment with different nut and fruit combinations to create your own unique heart-healthy dessert.

**Nutritional Benefits:**

- Walnuts and almond flour provide heart-healthy fats, while oats contribute heart-healthy fiber to this comforting dessert.

# 90. Walnut Brownies

**Prep Time:** 15 minutes | **Cooking Time:** 20 minutes | **Serving Size:** 12

## Ingredients

- 1/2 cup unsweetened apple sauce
- 1/4 cup coconut oil, melted
- 1/2 cup cocoa powder
- 3/4 cup whole wheat flour or almond flour
- 1/2 teaspoon baking powder
- 1/4 teaspoon salt
- 1/2 cup coconut sugar or maple syrup
- 1 teaspoon vanilla extract
- 1/2 cup walnuts, chopped
- Optional: dark chocolate chips

## Instructions

1. Preheat the oven to 350°F (175°C) and line a baking dish with parchment paper.
2. In a medium bowl, mix together the apple sauce, coconut oil, and cocoa powder until smooth.
3. In a separate bowl, combine the flour, baking powder, and salt.
4. Stir the dry ingredients into the wet ingredients, mixing just until combined.
5. Fold in the walnuts and chocolate chips if using.
6. Pour the batter into the prepared baking dish and spread it out evenly.
7. Bake for 18-20 minutes, or until a toothpick inserted into the center comes out clean.
8. Allow to cool before slicing into squares.

## Nutritional Information:

150 Calories - 20g Carbs - 8g Fat - 4g Saturated Fats - 3g Protein - 3g Fibers - 55mg Sodium - 10g Sugar

## Tip:

- For a gluten-free option, use almond flour or a gluten-free flour blend in place of whole wheat flour.

## Nutritional Benefits:

- Walnuts provide heart-healthy omega-3 fatty acids while the cocoa offers antioxidants beneficial for heart health.

# 91. Beat-Steady Banana Ice Cream

**Prep Time:** 10 minutes | **Cooking Time:** 0 minutes (2 hours freezing time) | **Serving Size:** 4

**Ingredients**

- 4 ripe bananas, sliced and frozen
- 1/2 teaspoon vanilla extract
- Optional toppings: dark chocolate chips, nuts, or berries

**Instructions**

1. Place the frozen banana slices in a food processor or high-speed blender.
2. Blend until smooth and creamy, scraping down the sides as needed.
3. Add the vanilla extract and blend again to combine.
4. Serve immediately for a soft-serve consistency, or transfer to a lidded container and freeze for 2 hours or until firm.
5. Garnish with your choice of toppings before serving.

**Nutritional Information:**

105 Calories - 27g Carbs - 0g Fat - 0g Saturated Fats - 1g Protein - 3g Fibers - 1mg Sodium - 14g Sugar

**Tip:**

- For a chocolate version, add 2 tablespoons of cocoa powder during blending.

**Nutritional Benefits:**

- Bananas are a good source of potassium, which is essential for heart health and maintaining a healthy blood pressure.

# 92. Earl Grey Tea Cakes

**Prep Time:** 15 minutes | **Cooking Time:** 20 minutes | **Serving Size:** 12

## Ingredients

- 1 cup whole wheat flour or almond flour
- 1/2 teaspoon baking powder
- 1/4 teaspoon baking soda
- A pinch of salt
- 1/4 cup coconut oil, softened
- 1/4 cup honey or maple syrup
- 2 large eggs
- 1/4 cup unsweetened almond milk or any plant-based milk
- 2 Earl Grey tea bags
- 1 teaspoon vanilla extract

## Instructions

1. Preheat the oven to 350°F (175°C) and line a muffin tin with paper liners or grease with a bit of coconut oil.
2. In a large bowl, whisk together the flour, baking powder, baking soda, and salt.
3. In a separate bowl, cream together the coconut oil and honey or maple syrup.
4. Beat in the eggs, one at a time, until well combined.
5. Heat the almond milk until warm, but not boiling. Remove from heat and add the tea bags. Allow to steep for about 5 minutes, then remove the tea bags, squeezing out any extra liquid.
6. Stir the tea-infused milk and vanilla into the wet ingredients.
7. Gradually add the wet ingredients to the dry ingredients, stirring just until combined.
8. Divide the batter evenly among the muffin cups.
9. Bake for 18-20 minutes, or until a toothpick inserted into the center comes out clean.
10. Allow to cool for a few minutes in the muffin tin, then transfer to a wire rack to cool completely.

## Nutritional Information:

100 Calories - 13g Carbs - 5g Fat - 3g Saturated Fats - 2g Protein - 2g Fibers - 70mg Sodium - 7g Sugar

## Tip:

- Experiment with different types of tea for a variety of flavors.

## Nutritional Benefits:

- Whole wheat or almond flour provides essential nutrients and fiber that are heart-healthy.

# 93. Sweet Potato Pudding

**Prep Time:** 15 minutes | **Cooking Time:** 0 minutes (requires chilling) | **Serving Size:** 4

## Ingredients

- 2 medium sweet potatoes, baked and cooled
- 1/4 cup unsweetened almond milk
- 2 tablespoons pure maple syrup or honey
- 1 teaspoon vanilla extract
- 1/2 teaspoon cinnamon
- 1/4 teaspoon nutmeg
- Optional toppings: chopped nuts, seeds, or a dollop of coconut whipped cream

## Instructions

1. Peel the baked sweet potatoes and place the flesh in a high-speed blender or food processor.
2. Add the almond milk, maple syrup, vanilla extract, cinnamon, and nutmeg to the blender.
3. Blend until smooth and creamy, adding a little more almond milk if necessary to achieve a pudding-like consistency.
4. Divide the pudding among four serving dishes and refrigerate for at least 2 hours, or until chilled.
5. Garnish with your choice of toppings before serving.

## Nutritional Information:

105 Calories - 25g Carbs - 0g Fat - 0g Saturated Fats - 1g Protein - 4g Fibers - 40mg Sodium - 10g Sugar

## Tip:

- For a more indulgent treat, blend in 2 tablespoons of unsweetened cocoa powder.

## Nutritional Benefits:

- Sweet potatoes provide essential vitamins and minerals, including heart-healthy potassium and vitamin A.

# 94. Peach and Berry Crumble

**Prep Time:** 15 minutes | **Cooking Time:** 45 minutes | **Serving Size:** 6

## Ingredients

- 4 ripe peaches, sliced
- 1 cup mixed berries (strawberries, blueberries, raspberries)
- 1 tablespoon lemon juice
- 1/2 cup oats
- 1/4 cup almond flour
- 1/4 cup coconut sugar or maple syrup
- 1/4 cup coconut oil, melted
- 1/2 teaspoon cinnamon

## Instructions

1. Preheat the oven to 350°F (175°C).
2. In a large mixing bowl, toss the sliced peaches, mixed berries, and lemon juice.
3. Transfer the fruit mixture to a baking dish.
4. In another bowl, combine the oats, almond flour, coconut sugar, coconut oil, and cinnamon. Mix well until crumbly.
5. Sprinkle the oat mixture evenly over the fruit in the baking dish.
6. Bake for 40-45 minutes, or until the fruit is bubbling and the topping is golden brown.
7. Allow to cool slightly before serving.

## Nutritional Information:

200 Calories - 30g Carbs - 10g Fat - 6g Saturated Fats - 3g Protein - 4g Fibers - 0mg Sodium - 20g Sugar

## Tip:

- Serve warm with a scoop of banana ice cream for an extra treat.

## Nutritional Benefits:

- Berries are packed with antioxidants, which are beneficial for heart health, while oats provide soluble fiber that can help lower cholesterol levels.

# 95. Kiwi Lime Sorbet

**Prep Time:** 10 minutes | **Cooking Time:** 0 minutes (2 hours freezing time) | **Serving Size:** 4

**Ingredients**

- 6 ripe kiwis, peeled and sliced
- Juice of 2 limes
- 2-3 tablespoons honey or maple syrup (adjust to taste)

**Instructions**

1. Place the sliced kiwis in a single layer on a baking sheet lined with parchment paper. Freeze for at least 2 hours, or until solid.
2. Once the kiwis are frozen, place them in a food processor along with the lime juice and sweetener.
3. Blend until smooth and creamy, scraping down the sides as needed.
4. Taste and add more sweetener if desired, blending again to combine.
5. Serve immediately for a soft-serve consistency, or transfer to a lidded container and freeze for an additional hour for a firmer texture.

**Nutritional Information:**

100 Calories - 25g Carbs - 0g Fat - 0g Saturated Fats - 1g Protein - 3g Fibers - 5mg Sodium - 18g Sugar

**Tip:**

- Garnish with a few fresh mint leaves or a sprinkle of coconut flakes for an extra touch.

**Nutritional Benefits:**

- Kiwi and lime are excellent sources of vitamin C, an antioxidant that supports heart health.

# 96. Hazelnut Gelato

**Prep Time:** 20 minutes | **Cooking Time:** 0 minutes (4 hours freezing time) | **Serving Size:** 4

**Ingredients**

- 2 cups unsweetened hazelnut milk
- 1/4 cup honey or maple syrup
- 1 teaspoon vanilla extract
- 1/2 cup roasted hazelnuts, chopped
- A pinch of sea salt

**Instructions**

1. In a mixing bowl, whisk together the hazelnut milk, sweetener, vanilla extract, and sea salt until well combined.
2. Pour the mixture into a shallow dish and freeze for 1 hour.
3. After 1 hour, take the dish out, stir in the chopped hazelnuts, and break up any ice crystals with a fork.
4. Return to the freezer and repeat the stirring process every hour for the next 3 hours.
5. Allow the gelato to sit at room temperature for 5-10 minutes before scooping and serving.

**Nutritional Information:**

150 Calories - 10g Carbs - 10g Fat - 1g Saturated Fats - 3g Protein - 2g Fibers - 20mg Sodium - 8g Sugar

**Tip:**

- Drizzle with a little dark chocolate for an extra treat.

**Nutritional Benefits:**

- Hazelnuts are a good source of heart-healthy fats and vitamin E.

# 97. Lemon Poppy Seed Muffins

**Prep Time:** 15 minutes | **Cooking Time:** 20 minutes | **Serving Size:** 12 muffins

## Ingredients

- 2 cups almond flour
- 1/2 cup coconut flour
- 1/4 cup honey or maple syrup
- Zest and juice of 2 lemons
- 3 large eggs
- 1/4 cup unsweetened almond milk
- 2 teaspoons baking powder
- 2 tablespoons poppy seeds
- A pinch of salt

## Instructions

1. Preheat the oven to 350°F (175°C) and line a muffin tin with paper liners.
2. In a large mixing bowl, combine the almond flour, coconut flour, sweetener, lemon zest, lemon juice, eggs, almond milk, baking powder, poppy seeds, and salt. Mix well until smooth.
3. Divide the batter evenly among the muffin cups.
4. Bake for 18-20 minutes, or until a toothpick inserted into the center of a muffin comes out clean.
5. Allow the muffins to cool in the tin for 5 minutes, then transfer to a wire rack to cool completely.

## Nutritional Information:

150 Calories - 10g Carbs - 10g Fat - 1g Saturated Fats - 5g Protein - 3g Fibers - 100mg Sodium - 8g Sugar

**Tip:**

- These muffins can be frozen for up to 3 months in an airtight container.

**Nutritional Benefits:**

- Almond and coconut flours provide a gluten-free and low-carb alternative to traditional flours, making these muffins a heart-healthy choice.

# 98. Tender Heart Tiramisu

**Prep Time:** 20 minutes | **Cooking Time:** 0 minutes (4 hours chilling time) | **Serving Size:** 6

## Ingredients

- 1 cup brewed decaffeinated coffee, cooled
- 1 tablespoon coffee liqueur (optional)
- 1 cup mascarpone cheese or coconut cream
- 1/4 cup honey or maple syrup
- 1 teaspoon vanilla extract
- 1 package of ladyfingers or gluten-free sponge cake slices
- Cocoa powder, for dusting
- Dark chocolate shavings (optional)

## Instructions

1. In a shallow dish, combine the cooled coffee and coffee liqueur (if using).
2. In a separate bowl, whisk together the mascarpone or coconut cream, sweetener, and vanilla until smooth.
3. Briefly dip half of the ladyfingers or sponge cake slices into the coffee mixture, then arrange in a single layer in a serving dish.
4. Spread half of the cream mixture over the ladyfingers, then repeat with the remaining ladyfingers and cream mixture.
5. Cover and refrigerate for at least 4 hours, or until chilled.
6. Before serving, dust with cocoa powder and garnish with dark chocolate shavings, if desired.

## Nutritional Information:

250 Calories - 25g Carbs - 15g Fat - 8g Saturated Fats - 5g Protein - 1g Fibers - 100mg Sodium - 15g Sugar

## Tip:

- Use decaffeinated coffee to keep this dessert heart-friendly.

## Nutritional Benefits:

- Opting for a coconut cream alternative and gluten-free cake can make this classic Italian dessert more heart-healthy.

# 99. Sweet Savory Fig Tart

**Prep Time:** 20 minutes | **Cooking Time:** 25 minutes | **Serving Size:** 8

## Ingredients

- 1 1/2 cups whole wheat or almond flour
- 1/4 cup cold unsalted butter or coconut oil
- 2-3 tablespoons cold water
- 8 fresh figs, sliced
- 1/4 cup crumbled goat cheese or vegan cheese
- 1 tablespoon honey or maple syrup
- A pinch of sea salt
- Fresh rosemary or thyme leaves for garnish (optional)

## Instructions

1. Preheat the oven to 375°F (190°C).
2. In a food processor, combine the flour and butter or coconut oil. Pulse until the mixture resembles coarse crumbs.
3. Add cold water, one tablespoon at a time, until a dough forms.
4. Press the dough into a tart pan, covering the base and sides evenly.
5. Arrange the sliced figs over the dough and sprinkle with crumbled cheese.
6. Drizzle with honey or maple syrup and a pinch of sea salt.
7. Bake for 20-25 minutes, or until the crust is golden and the figs are tender.
8. Allow to cool slightly before garnishing with fresh rosemary or thyme leaves, if using. Slice and serve.

## Nutritional Information:

180 Calories - 20g Carbs - 10g Fat - 5g Saturated Fats - 4g Protein - 4g Fibers - 80mg Sodium - 10g Sugar

## Tip:

- Serve warm, perhaps with a scoop of heart-healthy hazelnut gelato from the previous recipes.

## Nutritional Benefits:

- Figs are a good source of dietary fiber and antioxidants, promoting heart health.

# 100.    Lychee Sorbet

**Prep Time:** 15 minutes | **Cooking Time:** 0 minutes (4 hours freezing time) | **Serving Size:** 4

## Ingredients

- 2 cups fresh or canned lychees, drained
- 1/4 cup honey or maple syrup
- 1 tablespoon fresh lime juice

## Instructions

1. In a blender, combine the lychees, sweetener, and lime juice. Blend until smooth.
2. Pour the mixture into a shallow dish and freeze for 1 hour.
3. After 1 hour, take the dish out and break up any ice crystals with a fork.
4. Return to the freezer and repeat the stirring process every hour for the next 3 hours.
5. Allow the sorbet to sit at room temperature for 5-10 minutes before scooping and serving.

## Nutritional Information:

100 Calories - 25g Carbs - 0g Fat - 0g Saturated Fats - 1g Protein - 2g Fibers - 5mg Sodium - 20g Sugar

## Tip:

- Garnish with fresh mint leaves for an extra refreshing touch.

## Nutritional Benefits:

- Lychees are rich in Vitamin C, which supports heart health by protecting against oxidative stress.

# Chapter 9:    Meal Planning and Preparation

## Tips for meal prepping

Embracing a heart-healthy lifestyle goes beyond merely selecting the right ingredients; it's about incorporating a sustainable system that supports these choices daily. In today's fast-paced world, filled with demanding work schedules and personal responsibilities, the challenge often lies in the implementation. How do we ensure that every meal aligns with our health objectives without becoming overwhelmed?

Enter meal prepping, a strategic approach to food that is as much about organization as it is about nutrition. By setting aside a dedicated time each week to plan, shop, and prepare, you can transform your kitchen into a heart-healthy haven. This process involves batch cooking ingredients, portioning meals, and storing them in ways that retain their freshness and nutritional value. Not only does this method guarantee that you have consistent access to nutritious dishes, but it also alleviates the daily stress of wondering what to cook. Furthermore, by being deliberate in your meal preparation, you can manage portion sizes, reduce food waste, and ensure a varied and balanced diet.

Meal prepping is more than just cooking in bulk; it's about creating a systematic approach that aligns with your heart-healthy objectives. As we journey through this chapter, we'll uncover an array of techniques designed to optimize your meal prepping endeavors. These techniques range from efficient chopping skills to maximize nutrient preservation, to methods that speed up cooking times without compromising on taste.

Additionally, selecting the right tools can make a significant difference. We'll introduce you to essential kitchen gadgets that can simplify and enhance the preparation process, ensuring that you get the most out of your ingredients. But it's not just about the tools; it's about knowing how to use them effectively. Through step-by-step guidance, we'll demonstrate the best practices for using these tools, helping you become more adept in the kitchen.

The process also extends to post-cooking activities. How do you store your meals to ensure they remain fresh and retain their nutritional value? We'll explore various storage containers and the benefits they offer, from glass containers that prevent flavor transfer to vacuum-sealed options that prolong freshness. The art of portioning will also be covered, providing insights into how to measure meals that cater to your nutritional needs.

Creating a weekly menu is a cornerstone of effective meal prepping. Not only does it provide a clear structure, but it also ensures variety in your diet. We'll walk you through the process of crafting a balanced menu that incorporates all the essential food groups, offering templates and ideas to spark inspiration.

For those who are just beginning their meal prepping journey, fear not. We'll start with the basics, ensuring you have a strong foundation. For the seasoned meal preppers looking to elevate their skills, advanced tips and hacks await, designed to refine and enhance your process.

Ultimately, our goal is to make heart-healthy eating a seamless part of your lifestyle. With the right knowledge and practical techniques, you'll be better equipped to prepare meals that not only tantalize your taste buds but also nourish your heart. Embrace this journey with us, and let every meal be a testament to your commitment to heart health.

## Sample 28-day meal plan

The 28-day meal plan, carefully crafted within this book, is more than just a guide to heart-healthy eating. It's an invitation to embark on a diverse culinary voyage, ensuring that each day is flavored with innovation, freshness, and variety. As you navigate through this gastronomic journey, you'll encounter recipes that have been meticulously designed to offer both taste and nutritional benefits, underpinning the belief that heart-healthy meals can be a delightful fusion of flavors, textures, and aromas.

However, it's essential to underscore the importance of individual health needs. While this meal plan offers flexibility and variety, aiming to maintain daily sodium consumption around 1500 mg for those with high blood pressure concerns, everyone's body and health conditions are unique. If you have specific dietary restrictions, whether due to conditions like diabetes, allergies, or any other health concerns, it's imperative to approach this guide with caution and mindfulness.

Always remember, this cookbook serves as a general guideline, and while it emphasizes heart health, it might not cater to all specific health conditions. Before making any significant changes to your diet or if you intend to incorporate these recipes into your regular meals, it's crucial to consult with a healthcare professional—be it your doctor, dietician, or nutritionist. They can provide personalized advice, ensuring that the meals you consume are not only delicious but also tailored to support all aspects of your health and well-being.

Moreover, food is not just sustenance; it's an experience, a memory, and, most importantly, a key pillar of our health. As you delve deeper into this meal plan, remember to listen to your body, be aware of its reactions, and prioritize its needs. After all, the ultimate goal is holistic health, where the heart, body, and soul are all in harmonious sync.

Enjoy!

| Day | Breakfast | Lunch | Snack & Sides | Dinner | Dessert |
|---|---|---|---|---|---|
| 1 | Sunrise Berry Quinoa Bowl | Heartfelt Veggie-Packed Chili | Beat-Steady Baked Kale Chips | Veggie Loaded Chili | Heart-Sweet Berry Compote |
| 2 | Oatmeal with Berries | Tender Greens and Grains Bowl | Lemon Zest Popcorn | Lemon-Herb Chicken | Tender Heart Tiramisu |
| 3 | Nutty Banana Muffins | Harmony Quinoa Salad | Wholesome Heart Walnut Mix | Baked Salmon | Lemon Bars |
| 4 | Avocado Toast with Sunflower Seeds | Loving Pita Pockets | Heart-Happy Hummus | Chickpea Curry | Lavender Panna Cotta |
| 5 | Wholesome Heart Egg White Omelette | Roasted Veggie Bowl | Herb Roasted Nuts | Seafood Paella | Sweet Potato Pudding |
| 6 | Nutrient-Packed Spinach and Feta Wrap | Black Bean Soup | Lemon Zest Popcorn | Grilled Veggies Platter | Turmeric Pumpkin Pie |
| 7 | Tender Loving Care Bran Muffins | Nourishing Nicoise Salad | Wholesome Heart Walnut Mix | Heart's Embrace Eggplant Casserole | Hazelnut Truffles |
| 8 | Oat Pancakes | Heart-Wise Walnut Salad | Beat-Steady Baked Kale Chips | Veggie Loaded Chili | Lemon Bars |
| 9 | Cardio Kickstart Smoothie Bowl | Cardio-Careful Chickpea Salad | Lemon Zest Popcorn | Lemon-Herb Chicken | Peach and Berry Crumble |
| 10 | Morning Glory Granola | Olive Heart Mediterranean Wrap | Wholesome Heart Walnut Mix | Baked Salmon | Heart-Sweet Berry Compote |
| 11 | Omega-Boosting Chia Pudding | Vibrant Veggie and Hummus Wrap | Heart-Happy Hummus | Chickpea Curry | Hazelnut Gelato |
| 12 | Heartbeat Beetroot Smoothie | Edamame Bowl | Herb Roasted Nuts | Seafood Paella | Tender Heart Tiramisu |
| 13 | Breakfast Bars | Lemon Herb Chicken Salad | Lemon Zest Popcorn | Grilled Veggies Platter | Kiwi Lime Sorbet |
| 14 | Rise and Shine Nut Butter Bowl | Cardio-Care Cauliflower Rice Bowl | Beat-Steady Baked Kale Chips | Veggie Loaded Chili | Walnut Brownies |

| Day | Breakfast | Lunch | Snack & Sides | Dinner | Dessert |
|---|---|---|---|---|---|
| 15 | Heartful Hemp Seed Granola | Harmonious Vegetable Soup | Lemon Zest Popcorn | Lemon-Herb Chicken | Nutty Apple Crisp |
| 16 | Savory Breakfast Quiche | Lentil and Vegetable Stew | Wholesome Heart Walnut Mix | Baked Salmon | Heart-Sweet Berry Compote |
| 17 | Berry-Nut Yogurt Parfait | Heartfelt Veggie-Packed Chili | Heart-Happy Hummus | Chickpea Curry | Earl Grey Tea Cakes |
| 18 | Heart's Delight Veggie Omelette | Nourishing Nicoise Salad | Herb Roasted Nuts | Seafood Paella | Chocolate Avocado Mousse |
| 19 | Nutrient-Packed Spinach and Feta Wrap | Loving Pita Pockets | Lemon Zest Popcorn | Grilled Veggies Platter | Sweet Savory Fig Tart |
| 20 | Morning Glory Granola | Cardio-Careful Chickpea Salad | Beat-Steady Baked Kale Chips | Veggie Loaded Chili | Lemon Bars |
| 21 | Omega-Boosting Chia Pudding | Olive Heart Mediterranean Wrap | Lemon Zest Popcorn | Lemon-Herb Chicken | Hazelnut Truffles |
| 22 | Heartbeat Beetroot Smoothie | Vibrant Veggie and Hummus Wrap | Wholesome Heart Walnut Mix | Baked Salmon | Honey Almond Biscotti |
| 23 | Breakfast Bars | Edamame Bowl | Heart-Happy Hummus | Chickpea Curry | Lemon Bars |
| 24 | Rise and Shine Nut Butter Bowl | Lemon Herb Chicken Salad | Herb Roasted Nuts | Seafood Paella | Lavender Panna Cotta |
| 25 | Heartful Hemp Seed Granola | Cardio-Care Cauliflower Rice Bowl | Lemon Zest Popcorn | Grilled Veggies Platter | Heart-Sweet Berry Compote |
| 26 | Savory Breakfast Quiche | Harmonious Vegetable Soup | Beat-Steady Baked Kale Chips | Veggie Loaded Chili | Lemon Poppy Seed Muffins |
| 27 | Berry-Nut Yogurt Parfait | Lentil and Vegetable Stew | Lemon Zest Popcorn | Lemon-Herb Chicken | Tender Heart Tiramisu |
| 28 | Heart's Delight Veggie Omelette | Heartfelt Veggie-Packed Chili | Wholesome Heart Walnut Mix | Baked Salmon | Chocolate Avocado Mousse |

Discover exclusive Digital Bonuses accompanying this cookbook: a vibrant, full-color edition of this meal plan awaits. Print it, display it in your kitchen, and let it be your daily culinary compass.

# Chapter 10:   Beyond the Kitchen

## Tips for maintaining a heart-healthy lifestyle outside of the kitchen

Transitioning to a heart-healthy lifestyle is a holistic endeavor that sweeps beyond the cozy corners of your kitchen into the vast realm of daily living. It's about weaving heart-healthy practices into the fabric of your day, nurturing not only your heart but your overall well-being. Here's a more enriched guide to infusing heart-healthy choices into your daily routine, no matter where the day takes you:

1. **Embrace Regular Physical Activity:**

   - Exercise is the melody to which your heart dances in joy. Engage in activities that spark vitality within you, be it a brisk morning walk, a rejuvenating run, a serene swim, or a zestful Zumba session. The aim is to accumulate at least 150 minutes of moderate-intensity exercise per week, forming a rhythm that your heart cherishes.

2. **Mindful Eating Outside Home:**

   - Dining out need not derail your heart-healthy endeavors. Opt for grilled rather than fried, baked instead of battered, and steamed over sautéed. Assert your dietary preferences, and choose eateries that align with your heart-healthy aspirations.

3. **Stay Hydrated:**

   - Water is the elixir that keeps the rhythm of your heart harmonious. Personalize your hydration goals based on your body's needs and activity levels, aiming for a baseline of eight 8-ounce glasses of water daily, and adjust accordingly.

4. **Manage Stress Mindfully:**

   - Stress is akin to a discord in the symphony of your heart. Delve into meditation, yoga, or simple breathing exercises to restore harmony. Discover what anchors calmness in your being and integrate it into your daily routine.

5. **Prioritize Sleep:**

   - Sleep is the silent healer, cradling your heart in a restorative embrace. Aim for 7-9 hours of restful sleep, creating a serene sleeping environment and a consistent bedtime routine.

6. **Maintain Regular Health Check-ups:**

   - Tune into your heart's whispers through regular health check-ups. They provide invaluable insights, enabling timely interventions and fostering a dialogue with your healthcare provider to fine-tune your heart-healthy regimen.

7. **Foster Social Connections:**

   - The warmth of meaningful connections is a balm to your heart. Engage in social activities that resonate with you, nurture relationships that uplift you, and surround yourself with a supportive community that echoes your heart-healthy values.

8. **Educate Yourself:**

   - Ignite your curiosity and delve into a quest for knowledge. Stay abreast of the latest research, attend health workshops, and immerse yourself in books that empower you with the wisdom to make informed heart-healthy decisions.

9. **Avoid Tobacco and Limit Alcohol:**

   - Clear the clouds of tobacco smoke and limit the storm of alcohol to a drizzle. These substances, in excess, can rain havoc on your heart's health.

10. **Practice Gratitude:**
    - Amidst the hustle of the day, pause to bask in gratitude. It's the soft glow that illuminates your heart-healthy journey, magnifying the joy in every small victory and propelling you forward with a heart full of hope.

Incorporating these enriched tips into the fabric of your daily life can significantly bolster your heart-healthy lifestyle outside the kitchen. Every dawn heralds a fresh opportunity to make choices that are in harmony with your heart's health, nurturing a lifetime of wellness that echoes through the days and years ahead.

## Additional resources (websites, books, communities)

Navigating the path to a heart-healthy lifestyle is a journey best accompanied by reliable resources that can provide further insight, support, and inspiration. Here are some recommended resources:

1. **Websites:**
    - **American Heart Association (AHA)**: A reputable source for heart-healthy living guidelines, latest research, and heart disease prevention tips.
    - **WebMD Heart Health Center**: Offers a wealth of information on heart conditions, treatments, and lifestyle modifications for better heart health.
    - **Mayo Clinic Heart Disease Section**: Provides comprehensive information on heart diseases, diagnostic tests, and treatments.

2. **Books:**
    - **"Prevent and Reverse Heart Disease"** by Caldwell B. Esselstyn Jr. M.D.: A seminal book that explores the role of a plant-based diet in preventing and reversing heart disease.

3. **Communities:**
    - **Heart Health Support Groups**: Local or online support groups can provide a sense of community, share experiences, and offer support on your heart-healthy journey.
    - **Meetup Groups**: Discover local Meetup groups focused on heart-healthy living, cooking, and exercising together.
    - **Facebook Groups**: Online communities like "Heart Healthy Living" and "Heart-Healthy Recipes" on Facebook can be a great place to share recipes, tips, and encouragement with others on a similar journey.

These resources can serve as compasses guiding you through the myriad of information available, helping you make informed decisions, and providing a sense of community and support as you venture further into your heart-healthy lifestyle. The journey towards a heart-healthy lifestyle is enriched when shared with a supportive community, equipped with accurate information, and inspired by the experiences of others.

# Conclusion

Dear valued reader,

From the bottom of our hearts, thank you. Your choice to invest in the "Heart Healthy Cookbook for Beginners" signifies more than just a purchase—it represents your dedication to embracing a healthier, more vibrant life for yourself and those you care for. We genuinely appreciate the trust you've placed in us, and we are humbled to accompany you on this transformative culinary journey.

This cookbook, with its myriad of recipes and tips, was meticulously crafted, keeping in mind the diverse needs and lifestyles of our readers. Our ultimate aspiration has been to present you with a comprehensive guide that not only educates but also delights. We hope that as you've flipped through these pages, experimented with the recipes, and savored the results, you've felt a sense of empowerment, joy, and a renewed commitment to heart health.

The journey towards a heart-healthy lifestyle is ongoing, filled with discoveries, challenges, and victories. With every ingredient you choose, every meal you prepare, and every bite you relish, you're making a conscious decision to prioritize your health and well-being. It's a commendable endeavor, and we celebrate you for it.

Before we part ways, we have one humble request. If this book has enriched your cooking experiences, enlightened your understanding of heart health, and provided practical value in your daily life, we'd be truly honored if you could share your thoughts with a review on Amazon. Such feedback not only aids our continuous improvement but also assists potential readers in making informed decisions.

In conclusion, always remember that every step you take, no matter how small, is a stride towards a healthier heart and a more fulfilling life. Stay passionate, stay committed, and most importantly, relish the journey.

Your feedback is invaluable to us and to those considering embarking on this heart-healthy journey. If this cookbook has resonated with you and brought joy to your table, please consider sharing your insights with an honest review on Amazon. Together, we can inspire a larger community to prioritize their heart's well-being. Thank you for being an integral part of this mission!

With heartfelt gratitude, Avery Lynn Morgan

# Appendix

## Glossary

A glossary can be an invaluable resource for readers unfamiliar with specific terms or seeking a quick refresher. Here's a glossary tailored for the "Heart Healthy Cookbook for Beginners":

- **Antioxidants:** Molecules that help defend the body against harmful free radicals. They can be found in various foods, especially fruits and vegetables like berries, nuts, and spinach.

- **Arrhythmias:** Abnormal heart rhythms that can result from issues in the heart's electrical system. They range from harmless to life-threatening and may require medical intervention.

- **Atherosclerosis:** A degenerative condition where plaque, comprised of fat, cholesterol, and other substances, accumulates inside the arteries. This buildup can restrict blood flow, potentially leading to heart attacks or strokes.

- **Balanced Meals:** Meals crafted to ensure an appropriate intake of various nutrients. They often include a protein source, whole grains, vegetables, and healthy fats, contributing to overall health and wellness.

- **Cardiovascular System:** Comprising the heart and an intricate network of blood vessels, this system is responsible for pumping and circulating blood throughout the body, delivering essential oxygen and nutrients to tissues.

- **Cholesterol:** A waxy substance found in the bloodstream and cells. While necessary for building cells, too much bad cholesterol (LDL) can lead to heart disease.

- **Coronary Artery Disease (CAD):** A prevalent heart condition resulting from damaged blood vessels or plaque buildup, reducing blood flow to the heart muscle and potentially leading to heart attacks.

- **Detoxification:** The process by which the body eliminates or neutralizes toxins. Some foods, like beets and leafy greens, can support natural detox processes.

- **Dietary Fiber:** Essential for digestive health, fiber aids in bowel regularity and can help lower cholesterol levels. Found in fruits, vegetables, whole grains, and legumes.

- **Glycemic Index (GI):** A ranking of carbohydrates in foods based on how they affect blood sugar levels. Foods with a low GI are slower to raise blood sugar.

- **Healthy Fats:** Fats essential for body function, including omega-3 and omega-6 fatty acids. Sources include avocados, nuts, seeds, and olive oil.

- **Heart Failure:** Contrary to its name, it doesn't mean the heart has stopped working. Instead, it indicates the heart's inefficiency in pumping enough blood to meet the body's needs.

- **Herbs and Spices:** Used for flavoring, these plant-derived ingredients can also offer health benefits. Many have antioxidant properties and can aid in reducing sodium intake when used as salt alternatives.

- **Hypertension:** Chronic elevated blood pressure, often "silent" with no evident symptoms, can lead to severe health complications and increase the risk of heart disease, stroke, and more.

- **Inflammation:** A protective response by the body against harmful stimuli. Chronic inflammation can be harmful and has been linked to many diseases, including heart disease.

- **Iron:** A mineral crucial for producing red blood cells and transporting oxygen in the blood.

- **Lean Proteins:** These are low in unhealthy fats, especially saturated fats. Examples include fish, lean cuts of poultry, tofu, and legumes.

- **Legumes:** Plant-derived foods rich in protein and fiber. They're a heart-healthy alternative to some animal proteins and include lentils, beans, and chickpeas.

- **Macronutrients:** Fundamental nutrients required in significant amounts for overall health. They include carbohydrates (providing energy), proteins (essential for tissue repair), and fats (vital for hormone production).

- **Metabolism:** The chemical processes in the body responsible for maintaining life, including the conversion of food into energy.

- **Micronutrients:** Vital vitamins and minerals needed in minute quantities but are paramount for a plethora of bodily functions, from bone health to brain function.

- **Minerals:** Inorganic nutrients that play key roles in many biological processes. Examples include calcium, potassium, and magnesium.

- **Monounsaturated Fats:** Healthy fats found in olive oil, avocados, and certain nuts. They can help reduce bad cholesterol levels, potentially lowering the risk of heart disease.

- **Nutrient Labels:** Mandated by many governments, these labels on food packaging offer insights into the food's nutritional content, helping consumers make informed dietary choices.

- **Omega-3 Fatty Acids:** A type of polyunsaturated fat known for its heart-healthy benefits. Commonly found in fatty fish like salmon, flaxseeds, and walnuts.

- **Organic:** Refers to foods grown without synthetic pesticides, herbicides, and certain other treatments.

- **Phytonutrients:** Compounds found in plants that have been shown to have health benefits. Examples include the lycopene in tomatoes and the beta-carotene in carrots.

- **Portion Control:** A conscious effort to consume appropriate serving sizes, especially important in today's world of oversized portions, to maintain a balanced diet and healthy weight.

- **Processed Foods:** Foods that have been altered from their natural state for safety or convenience. Overconsumption can be detrimental to health.

- **Probiotics:** Beneficial bacteria that reside in the digestive system. They can be boosted by consuming foods like yogurt and fermented foods.

- **Saturated Fats:** Found primarily in animal products and some plant oils. Excessive intake can raise cholesterol levels, increasing the risk of heart disease.

- **Sodium:** An essential mineral that helps maintain fluid balance. However, excessive sodium intake, mainly from salt, can lead to hypertension.

- **Trans Fats:** Artificial fats created during food processing. Known to increase the risk of heart disease, stroke, and type 2 diabetes.

- **Valvular Heart Diseases:** Diseases affecting the heart's valves, which regulate blood flow in and out of the heart's chambers. Damaged valves can impact the heart's efficiency and overall blood circulation.

- **Vitamins:** Organic compounds vital for normal growth and nutrition. They are required in small quantities from the diet because they cannot be synthesized by the body.

- **Whole Grains:** Unlike refined grains, these retain all original components—bran, germ, and endosperm. Consuming whole grains, such as quinoa, oatmeal, and brown rice, can reduce the risk of several chronic diseases.

- **Zinc:** An essential mineral vital for immune function, DNA production, and cell division.

# SCAN HERE TO
# DOWNLOAD THE BONUSES

## SCAN ME

OR COPY AND PASTE THE URL:
## https://bit.ly/3tPpaZF

Made in United States
North Haven, CT
30 April 2024

51975546R00063